GO
A 40-Day Journey To The Never Reached

Published by
Assemblies of God World Missions
1445 N. Boonville Avenue
Springfield, MO 65802-1894

ISBN 978-0-578-51425-3

TABLE OF CONTENTS

INTRODUCTION

You are about to embark on a spiritual journey that took the disciples of Jesus from His resurrection to His ascension. There were exactly 40 days that our Savior walked on this earth during that time, and as we follow along with those who were with Him from the resurrection to the ascension one word jumps off the pages at us. It is the word GO. Surprisingly enough it is found 32 different times in that time period with eight different imperatives shouting the same thing to its readers—GO.

So, why was going so important to the Lord? And where is He telling us to GO? During these next 40 days, as you read and journey with us, our prayer is that the command of Christ to GO will be deeply implanted in your hearts. We believe the reason that GO is so often used is that the Christian walk was never meant to be stationary. We should be on the go, not just geographically but spiritually as well. As you walk with us on this 40-day journey, you will GO in, GO anyway, GO before and GO wait. Going will bring a new depth to your walk with Christ and yet His command to go will allow us to GO further, GO tell, GO quickly and GO together.

Our other prayer at Asia Pacific Missions is that the command to GO will take you to the never reached. These are the peoples of the world who have not only never heard the gospel in their lifetime or in past generations but in all of human history. Part of why the contributors to this book wrote with the passion and love for the lost that they did is because they love, and many of them live among, these never reached peoples. We are calling this book a journey to the never reached because we hope that after reading this 40-day devotional you will be inspired to Pray, Give or GO.

Jeff Hartensveld
Asia Pacific Regional Director
Assemblies of God World Missions

ACKNOWLEDGMENTS

Go: Forty Days With Jesus to the Never Reached is the product of an amazing team. They deserve the credit for everything excellent in this devotional. I'll take the credit for everything else.

Jeff Hartensveld, you dreamed the dream, pulled together the team and paid for it all. Through the entire process you have provided visionary leadership and encouragement to all. Thank you.

Leslie Thomas and Nicco Musacchio at Merge Business Solutions, you two provided great advice, key connections, branding and marketing savvy and a ton of work. Thank you.

Dawn Brandon and Tammy Bicket at Between the Lines Creative Services, you did an awesome job cleaning up and condensing the devotional submissions. Thank you.

Pastors, missionaries and laypeople came together to provide amazing devotional stories. They are an elite group of leaders, theologians and boots-on-the-ground practitioners. Chris Carter, Brandon Powell, Timothy Schmidt, Dan Betzer, Katie Benson, Josh Lovelace, Greg Mundis, Cari Hurst, Mike and Missy Towers, Alan Johnson, Sam Paris, Jonathan Lowrance, Mark Lehmann, Rebeka Zeiler, Dick Brogden, Joel Hoobyar: Your words have inspired and challenged me. Thank you.

Readers will notice that some devotionals have no byline. These unnamed contributors give their lives to live and work among the never reached in highly sensitive contexts. Mentioning their names, the names of their co-workers or where they serve could endanger their lives. Some names/places have been changed to protect those who live in the shadow of persecution. You know who you are. Though you may not be credited in these pages, God has taken note. Thank you! You are my heroes.

Bryan Webb

GO QUICKLY

Matthew 28:1-7 ----------------------------

Now after the Sabbath, toward the dawn of the first day of the week, Mary Magdalene and the other Mary went to see the tomb. And behold, there was a great earthquake, for an angel of the Lord descended from heaven and came and rolled back the stone and sat on it. His appearance was like lightning, and his clothing white as snow. And for fear of him the guards trembled and became like dead men. But the angel said to the women, "Do not be afraid, for I know that you seek Jesus who was crucified. He is not here, for he has risen, as he said. Come, see the place where he lay.

Then go quickly and tell his disciples *that he has risen from the dead, and behold, he is going before you to Galilee; there you will see him. See, I have told you." (ESV)*

Setting Things Right

By Chris Carter, Japan

The story of things set right can only ever begin in one place—the empty tomb.

The Cross is the sharpest knife. With it, God has split time itself in half. In the shadow of the Cross, one age ends, and another begins. Rent in the wake of the Cross, history stands divided—before and after. One age ends with words of apparent defeat on Jesus' lips: "It is finished." The next age begins in earnest with an angel's two commands: "Come and see," and "Go quickly!"

Standing firmly in the new age, we clearly see the significance of "It is finished." Redemption's work is done. Salvation has been won. The power of death stands defeated. That's how God makes an end of things gone wrong. But how does He make a beginning of setting things right?

The answer lies in one word—resurrection. For this reason, the story of things set right can only ever begin in one place—the empty tomb. And that's precisely where Matthew brings us in the last chapter of his Gospel:

The angel said to the women, "Do not be afraid, for I know that you are looking for Jesus, who was crucified. He is not here; he has risen, just as he said. Come and see the place where he lay. Then go quickly and tell his disciples: 'He has risen from the dead and is going ahead of you into Galilee. There you will see him.' Now I have told you." (Matthew 28:5–7, NIV).

As the scene unfolds, three women hear the good news of resurrection. But when it comes to the counterintuitive, paradigm-smashing, mind-blowing news of resurrection, hearing won't suffice. Thus, the angel bids them, "Come and see!" Come and experience the reality of resurrection for yourselves!

Here we see the entire mission of the Church in miniature. The experience that makes us God's people begins with a message: "He has risen." But understanding that message requires the empty tomb. It takes a first-person encounter with resurrection power. Through tasting resurrection, we are renewed inwardly by the same Spirit of God who raised Christ from the dead. God has not designed this experience for self-centered enjoyment, but as something to be shared. It comes with a command to go and tell a message—the message of resurrection. Therefore, in the experience of the women, we encounter the beginning of things being set right. In them, the Church's mission has already begun, for they are the first to hear and obey the command to "go!"

The angel has commanded the women to tell the news of the resurrection to Jesus' disciples. But he has just as strongly commanded them to do the telling in a particular way— "go quickly." In English, this looks like two separate commands: "Go quickly," and "Tell." But in Greek, going and telling are inextricably bound together. Without going, there is no telling; likewise, without telling, there is no going. Nonetheless, "telling" controls the sentence; going only has imperative force as the necessary precondition of telling.

For believers, the message always takes first priority. We do not go for the sake of going. We do not leave home to satisfy our wanderlust or sense of adventure. Just as the women were commanded to tell the message of resurrection to the disciples, we have been commanded to tell this same message to the world. It is a command to do all that it takes—no matter how difficult, dangerous, or inconvenient—in order to tell. Those who respond to the command to tell always begin by moving toward the lost. But being near those who need resurrection is not yet obedience. Mission done with the philosophy of "preach the gospel and, if necessary, use words" may meet the requirement of going. But no matter how bright our smiles or good our intentions, going without telling does not accomplish the mission we have been given.

The inseparable commands of going and telling herald the beginning of the new age of salvation. A new sense of urgency is captured in the adverb "quickly." But "quickly" is not primarily about speed. Matthew 28:8-9 says the excited women were running when they met Jesus on the way. They could not have run the whole time, nor did the angel expect them to do so. Indeed, the word translated "quickly" has more to do with priorities and single-mindedness than with speed. "Go quickly" means that every priority of life outside of going must take a back seat, as we ignore every distraction.

Responding to the command to go quickly won't make us track stars for Jesus. God called me to missions through a vision at age 17 and, later, to graduate school through a prophetic word. From call to the mission field took 12 years. For me, nothing about going was speedy. Instead, it required years of marching in one direction while ignoring all distractions. This is what it means to live in the new age in which resurrection power is setting things right. For Christians, obedience trumps everything. All the normal priorities of life have been reordered. For us, success, comfort, security, honor and fame mean nothing. They belong to the old age undone by the words on our Savior's dying breath: "It is finished." Now, as denizens of the new age, our lives are dominated by the values of that age, with its imperative to go and tell. We go quickly because, for us, nothing else matters. Go quickly!

ANSWER THE CALL

- In Matthew 28:19, Christ's Great Commission echoed the angel's command in verse 7 to go and tell. Does your life reflect this Christian imperative to go and tell?

_____

_____

_____

_____

_____

- Do your actions and attitudes demonstrate the priority of obeying Christ's command to go and tell? If not, what must you do to reorder your life and put God's call first?

_____

_____

_____

_____

_____

GO QUICKLY!

How can you better reflect the urgency of Christ's command?
Ask the Holy Spirit to help you analyze your priorities as revealed by your actions and attitudes. Recommit yourself to quickly obeying the Great Commission.

PRAY

Never Reached People Group: THE RAKHINE OF MYANMAR

Ask God to send more workers so that no Rakhine man, woman or child will remain never reached by the gospel.

Your Passion

By Brandon Powell, Thailand

Jesus invites you now to pick up where you left off.

What would it have been like to have been with the two Marys on their way to the tomb on that first Easter? They probably awoke with sorrow and many questions. But at Jesus' tomb an angel met them with words that made their hearts leap:

"He is risen from the dead, just as he said would happen. Come, see where his body was lying. And now, go quickly and tell his disciples that he has risen from the dead, and that he is going ahead of you to Galilee. You will see him there. Remember what I have told you" (Matthew 28:6–7, NLT).

Can you imagine their shift from mourning to sheer joy? This kind of shift naturally happens when someone decides to follow Christ. The good news of Christ's resurrection makes us want to tell someone—quickly.

As the women rushed to obey, they encountered Jesus. At first, they didn't realize it was Him. Despite their urgency to complete their task, Jesus pulled them aside for unhurried time with Him, knowing that was exactly what they needed before they continued their journey. This happens to us today. We may be filled with passion and urgency for going and doing, but Jesus often pulls us aside to focus first on being. Once we've spent time with our risen Lord, our witness is much more powerful and effective.

I was born in a hurry to get to the mission field. I believe God called me even before I was born. My mother said that while she was pregnant with me, the Holy Spirit spoke to her about my future in missions. One church service, I kicked in her belly whenever they sang the line, "Let every tribe and nation, with love and adoration, praise His holy name."

From the moment I felt called to missions, I wanted to go quickly. A few days after high school graduation, I hopped on a plane and spent the entire summer in Latin America doing street evangelism. That was such a special time, but I knew the Holy Spirit was leading me to get a college degree. It was hard to wait; I knew I was supposed to be on the mission field, and four years of school seemed like a long time. Still, my time at North Central University in Minneapolis was important. There, God opened my eyes to the people of Southeast Asia, many of whom have never heard the gospel. My world was changed, and my urgency increased when I spent time in Asia. I knew I wanted to take the gospel there, where it had never been preached.

Before I got to the field there were even more delays. Through our time abiding with Jesus, my wife and I knew He was leading us to pastor a church in Wisconsin. Although it was a difficult season, we can look back and see God's refining work in us and in others through our ministry. After what seemed like an eternity, though only four years later, we were approved as missionaries to Thailand.

While I didn't get to the field as fast as I'd hoped, I did ultimately step into what I believe God called me to do. And although I wish I had heeded advice to relax and enjoy each season of life, I don't regret the time I spent longing to be where my heart was. I believe two things helped me stay on track: that urgency I had for going and telling never reached people and my time abiding with Jesus.

I can list too many close friends who lost their passion for souls along the way. Some are no longer living for Christ. I believe that they failed to distinguish a brief God-ordained rest stop in which we encounter Jesus from a derailment that takes us totally off track. When we bypass the time God calls us to spend with Him, our urgency for reaching the lost fades. My encouragement to you is twofold.

First, always abide in Jesus. Abiding time with Jesus may take you to the wayside, along scenic paths, over mountains, and through scary, refining valleys. But that time is essential to what God is working in and through you.

Second, hold fast to the urgency of your commission to reach people everywhere for Christ. The scenic route is only for a season; don't get lost there. Are you staying where you are because it's sensible or comfortable? Or is this really the place the Holy Spirit wants you for this time? Do you have a call beyond where you are today?

Do you remember what Jesus told you? Ask the Holy Spirit to rekindle the passion and the urgency He planted in you—perhaps long ago. It's not too late. Jesus invites you now to pick up where you left off. Don't let age or circumstances keep you any longer from joining Jesus in this Great Commission. The risen Savior is calling—will you go?

ANSWER THE CALL

- When did you first feel God calling you to go and tell?

_____

_____

_____

_____

- Have you answered that call fully and quickly?

_____

_____

_____

_____

- What is the Holy Spirit speaking to your heart today?

_____

_____

_____

_____

GO QUICKLY!

Spend time asking God to guide you and give you wisdom. Don't rush through abiding time with Jesus—time in which God is preparing you to do and go. But be careful not to let your rest stop be your final stop. Recommit yourself to following God's leading every step of the way to fulfill His plan for your life.

PRAY

Never Reached People Group: SOUTHERN THAI MUSLIMS

Ask God to prepare the hearts of the Southern Thai Muslims for the coming of the gospel and the hearts of workers to go and tell them.

Doors of Opportunity

We must act quickly and not delay when even the smallest opportunity to share opens up.

Just one more day and his little boy would have died. For nine miles a worried father carried his severely burned 5-year-old son down a rugged mountain road, hoping our visiting team could save him. When we first saw him, the boy was dying. His scalded arm was scabbed over and oozed with infection. Quickly cleaning and dressing the wound, our medical team agreed: If the father had waited one more day, gangrene would have killed the boy.

We were gratified to help save his life—grateful for the rare opportunity to be within reach of this family just when their need was greatest. But we also desperately wanted opportunities to share the gospel with the never reached people groups in the region. This would be difficult. The communist government gave permission for our team to bring school supplies and medical treatment in this area just once a year. Official escorts followed us everywhere to ensure that we had no opportunity for evangelism.

Two days later, it was clear God had miraculously healed the boy. Amazingly, his burns had been replaced by healthy new pink skin. Not only did God snatch the boy from death and heal his arm, but He opened the father's spiritual eyes. While his spiritual life had been tied up in animistic worship of ancestors and animal sacrifices to the spirits of the land, God opened the door for him to hear, in one brief moment while the escorts were away, about our God who is both Healer and Savior. It was a lot for that father to process; he had never before heard the name of Jesus. But light shone in his eyes as he acknowledged that he must believe in this God because only the true God could heal his son.

The window was narrow, and the time was short. But because our team went quickly, God made a way to heal a dying boy and reveal himself to a man who had never heard the name of Jesus. We must act quickly and not delay when even the smallest opportunity to share opens up.

I believe that the instruction the angels gave to the women on that first Easter morning— "Go quickly and tell"—is meant for us today. The command is repeated in Matthew 28:19 in the Great Commission. Jesus wasn't just speaking to a select few. He was telling all of us—not just missionaries and preachers—to "go and make disciples."

My husband and I read this command and felt compelled to go quickly, even though we didn't feel equipped for the task. It sounded crazy to us that God would ask an auto mechanic and a high school math teacher to go to the mountains of this Southeast Asian country to tell people about Jesus.

God's call to us was similar to what He said to Moses, who was trying to get out of going to Egypt to proclaim God's deliverance to the enslaved Israelites. "What's in your hand?" God asked Moses (Exodus 4:2). "A shepherd's staff," Moses replied. Moses only had this one thing, and it seemed of little value. He was just a shepherd who knew how to live in the desert. Yet, those were skills God had intentionally developed in Moses, knowing they would be required to lead the Israelites through the desert to the Promised Land. We, too, trusted the Father to place in our hands every skill we would need for life and ministry in this remote place.

Since obeying God's command, God has used us to open an English and Skills Training Center for junior high and high school students. The skills God had already put in our hands were exactly what He used to build a platform that would engage the never reached of this Southeast Asian country. Our Heavenly Father specifically gifted us for the plans He has for us. Those gifts will be used for His glory when we surrender them to Him. The same is true for you.

Will you feel inadequate for the task the Father has laid out before you? Yes! But that will just bring God more glory, as His strength is made perfect in your weakness. Go anyway. Will you be afraid? Yes! But go quickly anyway. Matthew 28:8 says:

The women ran quickly from the tomb with fear and great joy (AMP).

That's a beautiful picture of what it looks like to step out in faith into the unknown. We stepped out in faith into an unknown land with an unknown language and culture and an uncertain future. Sure, we've felt fear, but we've also known great joy.

Ask God where He's leading you to share now before a window of opportunity closes. It might be reaching out to a neighbor or classmate. It could be building a relationship with someone in your own country who doesn't look or think like you. Or it might be launching out across an ocean to an unknown land to speak an unknown language to people who have never heard the gospel. No matter where God is leading you, He'll use the skills and gifts He has divinely given you. So, no more excuses. Someone is waiting to hear. Go quickly!

ANSWER THE CALL

- What skills or gifts has God given you that might seem outside the typical job description of a missionary? How might God use those gifts if you let Him?

_____

_____

_____

_____

_____

- What door has God opened to you to tell others about Christ?

_____

_____

_____

_____

_____

GO QUICKLY!

Make two lists: one of your skills and assets and one of your fears related to fulfilling God's call. Consecrate each asset to God, asking Him to use them for His glory. Commit each fear to God, asking Him to give you courage to obey in spite of your fears.

PRAY

Never Reached People Group: THE LAO PHUAN OF LAOS

Ask God to arrange for Lao Phuan individuals to have divine appointments with Christ followers, wherever they may go.

Perishable

By Bryan Webb, Area Director, Pacific Oceania

We cannot delay the harvest that's coming.

"Go quickly and tell his disciples that he has risen from the dead, and behold, he is going before you to Galilee; there you will see him. See, I have told you" (Matthew 28:7, ESV).

Early Sunday morning, the two Marys went to the tomb to anoint the body of Jesus. Following the stunning announcement that Christ had risen from the dead, the angel next commanded them to "Go Quickly." Simply put, there is an urgency to our telling. The angel's instruction reveals that there is a perishable nature to the harvest, we are given a short window of opportunity for going and telling.

Have you ever gone to pour milk over your cereal and, instead of the milk flowing in a nice smooth arc, it comes out clump, clump, clump? A cursory sniff reveals a foul odor. A closer look at the milk jug reveals the problem. It's written there in black: Best by...followed by a date that passed two weeks ago.

Examine yourself carefully: There is no best-by date tattooed anywhere on you. Still, as the Bible assures us, "It is appointed for man to die once, and after that comes judgment" (Hebrews 9:27, ESV). We all have an expiration date.

Every person you interact with—family, co-workers, neighbors, even strangers in the supermarket—will live forever. Each one will spend eternity either with God in heaven or perishing in an eternal hell. You and I have a finite amount of time to influence them and attempt to affect where they will spend eternity.

For each, one day will be the last day we ever get to tell them about Jesus. This is true of those you interact with daily. But do you realize that 2 billion people in this world have no one who speaks their language who can tell them about Christ? If told, some of them would believe. This gives incredible urgency to our charge to go quickly and tell them before it's too late.

As a Bible school student, I carried a full academic load, worked a full-time job, and pioneered a cross-cultural church that required me to learn a second language and culture. Simply put, I was busy. Crazy busy. Way too busy. One day at work, a young man approached me. "John" lived at the center of the local party scene. He was friendly, humorous, and very popular. He had a quick smile, quick wit, and was quick to help anyone in need.

Leaning on a broom handle, John told me, "You know, Bryan, I've tried everything—drugs, alcohol, and women. Something is still missing in my life. I think I need to try this Jesus thing. Could you come over to the house on Saturday and explain things to me?"

What an opportunity! "Of course," I answered.

That Saturday, I found myself engaged in a marathon marriage crisis counseling session with a couple in our new church plant. The day passed without an opportunity to visit John. The following Monday I apologized profusely. John brushed it off. "No prob," he told me. "But do you think you could swing by this Sat?" he asked earnestly.

"Of course," I promised. "Next Saturday."

For three weeks, I found myself tied up every Saturday in inescapable situations. At work, I apologized repeatedly to John. I invited him to church and promised repeatedly: "Yes, next Saturday I will be free. Sure, I would love to talk to you about Jesus. No, really, I do want to, but it has been crazy busy. You understand."

John would smile and assure me that it was no big deal. "Just when you get the chance," he would answer.

On the fourth Monday, John wasn't at work. Jokes were made about how hard he must have partied that weekend. Tuesday, John didn't show up either, and joking turned to concern. Our employer had a firm points system regarding absences, and by missing two days in a row, John was getting perilously close to termination.

Tuesday night after work, one of his friends went to his house to check on him. The door was locked, and there was a note on the door. "Don't worry about me. I've decided to take a long trip." Feeling ominous about John's cryptic note, the friend forced open the door and discovered John dead—he had taken his own life.

I think of John often. Would things have been different had I visited him? I don't know. I will never know. I don't look forward to the conversation Jesus and I will have one day about John and my missed opportunity. I wish—oh, how I wish—I had gone quickly and told John all about Jesus, how He died for John's sins, rose from the dead, and today sits at the Father's right hand praying for us. Would John have believed? I don't know, but he would have had the opportunity.

I'll never get those Saturdays back, though I wish I could. If only I had one more chance—but I don't. You see the nature of our harvest? It's perishable. We must tell each person we encounter today about Christ. Tomorrow? It may be too late. We cannot delay the harvest that's coming. Whether through our faithfulness we reap a good harvest or lose the harvest, we must go quickly.

ANSWER THE CALL

- Have you been putting off what God is calling you to do today?

_____

_____

_____

_____

_____

- Choose to be mindful of both the perishable and eternal nature of those you interact with today.

_____

_____

_____

_____

_____

GO QUICKLY!

If you're having trouble distinguishing between the urgent and the important in your life, consider this: If at the end of this day/week/month you were going to face God and give an account of your work, how would you spend your time? What would be most important to God?

PRAY

Never Reached People Group: THE TAUSUG OF THE PHILIPPINES

Ask God for a spiritual breakthrough among the Tausug that would dispel centuries of spiritual darkness with the light of the gospel.

Every Minute Counts

By Timothy Schmidt, Pastor, Calvary Christian Church,
Lynnfield, Massachusetts

Why didn't you come sooner?

It was the first day of the week, and some grieving women had gathered around the tomb of their dearly beloved friend, Jesus Christ, who had been crucified just days before. To their surprise, they were met by an angel, who told them that Jesus had risen from the dead! He then gave them the specific instruction:

"Go quickly and tell his disciples that he has risen from the dead."
(Matthew 28:7, ESV).

The women immediately obeyed; they "departed quickly from the tomb with fear and great joy, and ran to tell his disciples" (v. 8). Their fear and joy were multiplied, however, as Jesus himself met them along the way. After falling at His feet in reverence and worship, they heard basically the same instruction from Jesus: Go and tell (v. 9).

The directive given by the angel and Jesus following His resurrection is still a fundamental instruction to all who call themselves followers of Christ. We are to "go and tell," sharing the good news that Jesus Christ has risen from the dead—and we must do it quickly! The women didn't hesitate or delay but simply obeyed what they had been told to do. They carried out their instruction with passion and purpose, making it the very priority of their lives.

Which begs the question: Can the same be said of us today? Is there a "go quickly" aspect to the nature and way in which we share the gospel with others? Or, is sharing the gospel something we say we are committed to doing but just never seem to get around to? Are we lacking the passion and purpose demonstrated by these women, who were privileged to be the first to tell the good news? Is it possible that, when Jesus asks us to go quickly, He is not only addressing the pace at which we carry the gospel, but the priority that it should carry in our hearts and lives as well?

Never is the need for urgency and priority in sharing the gospel seen more clearly than when someone is dying. When a church parishioner has an unsaved loved one sick and dying at the hospital, they will frequently ask me, as their pastor, to go and share the gospel. They don't want me to go talk to their loved one about our great church. They don't want me to share about our new building program or the new beautiful bus we just bought. They're not interested in me telling their loved one about all the ministries of the church or even the Christmas play that is coming. No, they want me to share one thing with their dying loved one—one thing and one thing alone, the main thing—the gospel of Jesus Christ. In fact, they are counting on me, depending on me to do this one thing. And they want me to get to that hospital as quickly as possible!

The reality is that people are dying all around us. None of us has as much time as we think. And while many well-intentioned Christians spend lots of time discussing and even debating when our Lord will return, the reality is that He will return today for many, as they take their last breath on earth. Someone in your family is dying today, someone in your neighborhood, someone at work, or someone at your school. The Lord is counting on you to follow His directive to go—quickly—and tell.

More than 100,000 people will die today— from America to Zimbabwe and everywhere between. Many will die without Christ. The urgency to go quickly and tell has never been greater, as demonstrated by the testimony of one missionary to Haridwar, India, near the Ganges River. Every year, millions of Hindus travel to this river by foot, train, bullock carts, and buses to bathe in the polluted waters of the Ganges. They hope that in washing themselves, they will find forgiveness for their sins. As this missionary was telling people about Jesus, he noticed a young woman sitting by the river bank, pounding her chest, and weeping uncontrollably. "Why are you weeping?" he asked her.

She replied, "My husband is sick. He cannot work. To find forgiveness for my sins and solutions to the problems of my home, I've given the best offering I can to Goddess Ganges—my only son, my 6-month-old baby boy. I just threw him into the river."

The stunned missionary gathered his composure and began to share the gospel with the distraught mother. He told her that God had given His only Son, Jesus Christ, so that she could be forgiven. He assured her that God was not angry with her but loved her very much. She wiped the tears from her eyes and looked earnestly into the eyes of the missionary. "I have never heard this before," she said sadly. "If only you had come to me half an hour sooner. I didn't have to kill my child. Why didn't you come sooner?"

Let us hear the call and commission of Jesus Christ once again to go quickly and tell others. Every minute counts.

ANSWER THE CALL

- God grieves like that mother when the chance to hear comes too late to save one of His children. What can you do today to avoid this tragic result?

_____

_____

_____

_____

_____

- What have you put off doing—giving to missions, praying, going— that might delay someone from having their chance to hear?

_____

_____

_____

_____

_____

GO QUICKLY!

Don't delay! God has put that burden on your heart for a reason. Pray! Give! Go! Speak! Whatever God has called you to do today, do it today.

PRAY

Never Reached People Group: THE TUGUTIL OF INDONESIA

Ask God for a mighty move of the Spirit among the Tugutil people that will open the hearts of many to Christ in your lifetime.

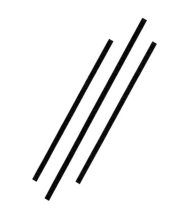

GO TELL

Matthew 28:8-10

So they departed quickly from the tomb with fear and great joy, and ran to tell his disciples. And behold, Jesus met them and said, "Greetings!" And they came up and took hold of his feet and worshiped him. Then Jesus said to them, "Do not be afraid; **go and tell my brothers** *to go to Galilee, and there they will see me." (ESV)*

A Church With a Heart for Missions

By Dan Betzer, Pastor, First Assembly of God, Fort Myers, Florida

Passion to tell the story of Jesus to those who have never heard is contagious.

When it's spring, you can find me in Israel. In the early 1970s, a friend of mine administered the Garden Tomb (thought by many to be where Jesus' body was laid for three days). One year, he agreed to let me go alone to the grave at 4 a.m.; I wanted to experience the mindset of Mary and the others on Resurrection morning.

Today, an iron grate keeps tourists from breaking off pieces of the rock bier where Jesus may have lain. But in the 70s, anyone entering the small tomb had access.

I sat in darkness and waited for the sun to rise behind the Mount of Olives. In my imagination, I could see Mary and her friends carefully wending their way to the tomb with anointing spices. But there was no body for them to anoint—only a living, resurrected King of Glory. His message to the trembling women still reverberates in the heart of every Spirit-filled believer:

"Be not afraid: go tell my brethren that they go into Galilee, and there shall they see me" (Matthew 28:10, KJV).

The command is still pertinent: Go tell the world! It is repeated often in the New Testament.

How did the women respond? They promptly obeyed Jesus' command. They had come to worship, but how valid is worship without obedience? In John 14:15, Jesus said, "If ye love me, keep my commandments." How can professing believers sing worship choruses yet refuse to support missions?

People often say to me, "I understand the importance of global evangelism, and I am praying about it!" Really? Praying about it? Think of a father telling his young son, "Junior, go upstairs and clean your room," only to hear the child say, "Father, I'll pray about it."

Obedience requires faith—a lot of it. For decades now, I've preached faith and missions to our congregation. We are the supply route, in effect, for our troops on the front line. Without us, they have a hard time winning the battle. So, on the last week of our annual missions convention, the "motor of our church," we receive faith promises for the coming year. In our church, 75 percent of all missions funds received go to missionaries on the field. The other 25 percent goes to purchase equipment for missionaries or to build churches overseas.

We never take missions money from the general fund. Malachi makes it clear that the tithe is for "the storehouse," the place where the believers are fed and sustained. Taking a percentage of tithe for missions sounds like a good idea...but is it? This immediately limits the amount people give to global evangelism. Our goal is to send to missionaries the same amount we spend in our church.

Last year, 77 missionaries spoke to our congregation from the pulpit. How can people truly understand what is happening overseas unless they hear the story from those living it—the missionaries themselves? We take an offering for each of those missionaries, and they receive 100 percent of what comes in. Over the course of a year, that's a considerable amount of money. In addition, funds come in each week from those who've made a missions faith promise. This giving principle has brought folks into our church who have been searching for a church devoted to missions.

Our missions emphasis involves everyone. Every year, several adult teams from our church fund their own short-term missions trips. For the past two years, our children have brought in more than $200,000 for missionaries. They give from allowances, work odd jobs in their neighborhoods, and ask those with funds to give. Over the past 30 years in this church, God has called some of those children to go tell, and they have obeyed. Our teens and college students are also hearing God's call to missions. Their response is genuine and enthusiastic.

This world view—passion to tell the story of Jesus to those who have never heard—is contagious. People respond in ways that push our prayer, giving, and going to a whole new level.

Fear keeps us from obedience. Rather than doing what Jesus commanded, we moan, "How will I pay my bills? Where will I get the funds?" But, as Jesus told the women at the tomb, "Don't be afraid!" Just before His ascension, Jesus reminded His disciples that signs and wonders would follow obedience to His directive. Those signs and wonders rarely precede obedience.

How can we be so sure God will empower and provide for us as we reach out to the world's lost? Jesus told His followers:

"All power is given unto me in heaven and in earth. Go ye therefore, and teach all nations, baptizing them in the name of the Father, and of the Son, and of the Holy Ghost: Teaching them to observe all things whatsoever I have commanded you: and, lo, I am with you alway, even unto the end of the world" (Matthew 28:18–20, KJV).

Jesus said He would be with us and provide for us for the whole journey. That's how we can be sure. And that's why we will obey.

ANSWER THE CALL

- What is Christ saying to you about missions today? How are you answering Christ's command to go and tell? What more can you do?

_____

_____

_____

_____

_____

- What role has your church played in fanning your flame of passion for the lost? How did you catch the passion for the world's lost? What can you do to help others catch that passion?

_____

_____

_____

_____

_____

GO TELL!

Share your passion for missions and your burden for the lost with another individual or group. Mentor a relative. Share missionary stories with your Sunday School class. Explain to your garage sale customers why you're giving a portion of your proceeds to missions projects. If you think about it, you'll come up with many opportunities.

PRAY

Never Reached People Group: THE KHALKA OF MONGOLIA

Pray for believers at work among the Khalka, that they and their families may have wisdom, courage, stamina, provision, favor, and grace as ambassadors of Christ's love.

The Power of the Spoken Word

God has given us a voice. He has given us stories to share and people to reach. He has commanded us to go and tell them.

There's nothing like being in a country where you don't speak the language to make you appreciate the power of the spoken word. As a missionary, it didn't take long to realize that to fulfill the purpose for which God had called us—to take the gospel to never reached people—we needed to be fluent in their language. We could be kind, hospitable, friendly, and compassionate, but without words, these people would remain never reached because the missionaries living next door were tongue-tied.

This became clear our first Christmas in a communist, Buddhist nation. Our children and I had crafted homemade snowflakes, ornaments, and a nativity scene from toilet paper rolls. It was a meager attempt to create some Christmas cheer, but our halls were decked more than the whole town put together. Our teenage neighbor came over one day, and her eyes lit up when she saw the decorations. She asked what they were for. I asked if she knew what Christmas was, and she said no. My heart pounded. With just four months in the country and little language under my belt, I knew I couldn't adequately explain Christmas to her, but I had to try. So, I said, "Christmas is a celebration of Jesus' birthday."

"Who is Jesus?" she asked.

For the first time in my life, someone was in my home who had never heard of Jesus. The gravity of that hit me hard. I tried to explain the Christmas story. As my best efforts fell embarrassingly short, the Lord reminded me the necessity of being able to effectively communicate the gospel with words. Good intentions do not change lives; the power of the gospel shared with clarity and conviction does.

Romans 10:14 clearly explains why the spoken message is necessary:

How, then, can they call on the one they have not believed in?
And how can they believe in the one of whom they have not heard?
And how can they hear without someone preaching to them? (NIV).

Although lives lived to the glory of God can be a testimony, people cannot come to faith in Christ unless we explain how. Our neighbor would never have known who Jesus is if we hadn't told her. The lost cannot be changed by the power of the gospel unless they hear it.

After this encounter, I knew I must prepare for future opportunities. This took time, effort, study, practice, and prayer. I had to relearn sharing the gospel in a new language and context. I had to think about how the gospel would be received and what emphasis might be needed to be culturally relevant in this country. Effectively telling people about Jesus takes intentional and purposeful preparation. Jesus used parables and culturally relevant stories. We must commit to intentionally prepare to share the gospel with our audience in mind.

Although there were other instances during our first term overseas when I found my language skills sorely lacking when I longed to speak effectively and freely about Jesus, I learned something. When we are willing to tell others about Christ, the Holy Spirit is faithful to do what we cannot. He empowers our humble efforts and simple words. We don't have the luxury of waiting until we feel completely ready to tell others about Jesus. We must feel the urgency of multitudes on their way to eternity separated from God. We must "make the most of every opportunity" (Ephesians 5:16).

One day, a friend shared her struggle with her drug-addicted son and its toll on her family. My language had improved, but I still wasn't confident in my ability to say everything I wanted to say. However, I wasn't going to pass up this God-ordained opportunity to witness to my friend. I told her about my family's similar struggle with my sister's addiction. Praise God, my sister's wanderings had led her back to Jesus, who radically changed her life. In telling my friend this story, we connected in a new way; Jesus became not just a foreign name to her, but someone who transforms lives. I didn't explain everything clearly, but I believe that God used my words to reveal a new part of himself to my Buddhist friend. Could I have shown the love of Jesus to her by simply being compassionate and understanding? Of course. But would she have walked away with a greater understanding of who God is and a desire to know Him more? No. Some things just can't be conveyed without words.

God has given us a voice. He has given us stories to share and people to reach. He has commanded us to go and tell. We are foolish if we think that the Great Commission can be fulfilled without the verbal proclamation of the gospel. In a world where more than one-third of the population has never heard the good news, we must be intentional in our preparation and presentation of the gospel message. We must take that message to the ends of the earth, where there are still many who cannot believe in Jesus because they have never heard His name. All believers are responsible for telling this generation about Jesus. This includes me and you. The time for being tongue-tied is over. Jesus is asking you to tell His story. Will you?

ANSWER THE CALL

- Jesus has commanded us to go and tell. To whom is God sending you?

_____

_____

_____

_____

_____

- What barrier do you need to overcome to effectively share the gospel with those God has called you to tell? What steps will you take?

_____

_____

_____

_____

_____

GO TELL!

Ask God to help and guide you as you make an intentional plan to overcome whatever is holding you back from telling others. Are you shy? Fearful? A poor speaker? Is there no one around you who hasn't heard? What are the first steps to building new friendships, preparing yourself, or overcoming your fears? Commit to readying yourself to go and tell. Ask God to help you.

PRAY

Never Reached People Group: THE BAMAH OF MYANMAR

Ask God to reveal himself to the Bamah people through dreams and visions.

An Unlikely Candidate

There is great diversity in the kind of people God uses to tell His story.

My family's life in Vietnam began in the summer of 2008, when God undeniably called us to leave our ministry positions and jobs in the States and move here. The primary focus of our work in Northern Vietnam is training local pastors, church planters and evangelists. We're often called on to preach at events for the Vietnamese Assemblies of God General Council and various district councils throughout the country. We preach at evangelistic outreach events, Bible school graduations and chapel services, dedication ceremonies for churches and training centers, and leadership and revival conferences. If you look at my life from the outside, you might guess that God's call to preach and teach was always clearly affirmed to me, but that's simply not the case.

In my early teenage years, various young people in our church youth group acknowledged the Lord's call on their lives. Visiting ministers and evangelists often affirmed the call of different group members. Many, my younger brother included, had natural attributes that fit well with the ministry. My brother was practically born preaching. When he was 5 years old, he would stand on the front porch of our rural home in central Texas and preach to the empty front yard and baptize my sister's cat or one of our chickens. He had it; he knew it, others knew it, and he has faithfully lived out the call to preach the gospel since his youth.

But my story was totally different—no prophetic words from others, no recognizable ministry attributes, nothing. I don't recall one person ever saying, "Someday God's going to use you to preach the gospel." The truth is, in my early teen years, I didn't see it in myself, nor did I have any desire to be a minister or missionary. I was shy and not good with words, with no inclination to be in front of people. At age 16, however, things began to change. That year, I was baptized in the Holy Spirit with the evidence of speaking in other tongues. Soon I began to feel broken for the spiritually lost and an inexplicable and inextinguishable desire to preach the Word of God.

I told the Lord, "I can't preach. I'm not that 'type'...and furthermore, NO ONE expects that from me!" As a compromise, and in response to the Lord's leading, I began to give financially to missions. Preaching, however, was a different story. Even though I had this stirring in my soul, my flesh struggled against the Lord's call for two more years. Finally, during a series of revival services at my dad's church, the Lord said "I'm not really looking for a preacher; I'm looking for someone who will surrender to Me and who is willing to tell the story. If you'll surrender to Me, I'll make you who I want you to be."

----
*You don't
get a pass
just because
it's not your
comfort zone.*

Almost 20 years ago, during that revival, I shocked myself—and I'm sure everyone in our little church—by responding to a "call to preach" altar call and publicly declaring God's call on my life to preach. God has always called men and women to be the medium through which His message is proclaimed. Jesus commissioned us to go tell! Jesus said, "This gospel WILL BE PREACHED in all nations." God has chosen to save those who would believe through the foolishness of PREACHING. The apostle Paul tells us that people can only believe in Jesus if someone tells them the story. Telling God's story is not optional in the divine plan of humanity's redemption.

However, there is great diversity in the kind of people God uses to tell His story. In the Bible, we find young people like Jeremiah and old men like Abraham. Some are well educated, like Luke and Paul, or uneducated, like Peter and John. We meet timid men, like Timothy, and bold women, like Deborah. There are fiery people, like John the Baptist, and stuttering introverts, like Moses. And then there's me—the bashful, introverted, unlikely candidate God still called to tell His story. When I look at my call to preach, I am reminded of Paul's words to the Corinthians:

God has not chosen many wise, powerful or noble, but God chooses the foolish [unlikely] to confound the wise (1 Corinthians 1:27).

Perhaps you've felt the Holy Spirit's calling you to go tell—to proclaim the gospel somewhere in the world. Maybe like me, however, you've disqualified yourself for one reason or another. Maybe someone else has helped you feel you aren't really the go-tell type. But you don't get a pass just because it's not your comfort zone. God is looking for surrendered people who will obey. As the Holy Spirit reminded me as a teenager, God's not really looking for talent, charisma, or finesse. He's looking for surrendered hearts of those willing to faithfully tell His story. The main character of the story that we are called to tell is the One who calls men and women into His service. He knows exactly what He's doing and the kind of person He can use. In our world today, an estimated 4 billion people have never heard a clear presentation of the gospel. Many of these people are eager to believe and call on the name of the Lord—if only someone would go and tell them. Will you let God use you? Will you go tell?

ANSWER THE CALL

- Do you have characteristics or deficiencies that make you feel disqualified for telling God's story at home or abroad? Are any of them more important than a willing and surrendered heart?

_____

_____

_____

_____

_____

- Have you surrendered to God's will for your life? If not, how long will you hold back?

_____

_____

_____

_____

_____

GO TELL!

Talk to a trusted spiritual friend or mentor about the spiritual battle in your soul over surrendering to God's call. Pray together, asking God to clarify His call and open your eyes to His plan for you.

PRAY

Never Reached People Group: THE TAY OF NORTHERN VIETNAM

Pray for miracles, signs, and wonders among the Tay people that will point them to our powerful God who loves them.

Upended

By Katie Benson, Indonesia

What a privilege it is to be a mouthpiece of the Lord to a nation that is far from Him.

My plans were upended in a moment. In a noisy chapel service at Central Bible College, I heard a still, small voice saying, "Will you go? Will you tell them about Me?" Suddenly, everything made sense. This was what I was made to do. I wanted to go to the mission field, and I wanted to tell people about Jesus! I was so confident that this was from God, I immediately changed my major to intercultural studies. I wanted to know all that I could, but I had no focal point. The call of others seemed more specific. Many had known for years exactly where God would send them. I wanted to know right then too. Uncertainty soon made me fearful and anxious. What if I'd heard God wrong? The unknown became a scary place.

I began telling God what I wanted. I told Him the places I would go. Then I found myself telling Him the places I would not go and the people I would not minister to. "I will go anywhere but Asia and tell anyone but Muslims," I told God. "Not there. Not them. I know nothing about Asia or Islam. I don't want to walk into the unknown." I would answer God's call, but I wanted to do so in a familiar place where I was comfortable and safe.

In 2013, all I needed to graduate were a few classes and an internship. I e-mailed people all over the world, not really caring at that point where I would go. I could go anywhere for just two months. Did you guess where I ended up interning? In Indonesia, a Muslim nation in Asia!

Before going, I was assigned books about Islam. Reading them, my heart began to break. I asked questions and wrestled with God. Is this really how it is? I wondered. How can people treat women this way? My heart began to soften for these people. I wanted to go to them. I wanted to be feet on the ground and tell them of His great love for them. I found that as I learned more, a passion and a burden was forming.

In the summer of 2014, I set foot in Indonesia for the first time. That first day was not ideal. I had a meeting with students that was marked by language confusion, cultural blunders, witchcraft, and a really late night. I retreated to the home where I was staying and cried. I cried a lot. This was harder than I imagined. None of this was what I had expected. Why was I here? It was so dark. The people felt too far from God. In my crying, I began to ask God for a bigger heart for these people. I saw the brokenness of the girls I met with. Brokenness was all around me. That first night, God began to deal with me.

> *Don't let the fear of the unknown keep you from answering the call to go and tell...*

Over the next few weeks, I fought with God and made a list of excuses as to why I wouldn't commit to this place. It was too soon. It was a big decision, and I shouldn't make it lightly. I wanted to get married and pay off loans first. I wanted to help my family take care of my mom, who was extremely ill. I needed to gain experience first. But each day, I found myself falling more in love with Indonesia, the people, and the culture. I loved the ministry here and took great joy in serving.

A week before I was to return to the States, the missionaries I was serving with asked me to consider returning to Indonesia. I said I'd pray about it. I was already praying. I knew the answer. God had been speaking to me the entire two months. I thought back to that moment in chapel when God spoke and said, "Will you go? Will you tell them about Me?" That week, I found myself surrendering all my excuses, fears, and desires to God and saying "Yes, I will go to Indonesia."

Four years later, I'm still ministering in Indonesia. The unknown went from being a scary place to a place of joy and excitement. I wake up and look forward to going each day and telling people about Jesus. What a privilege it is to be a mouthpiece of the Lord to a nation that is far from Him.

Don't let the fear of the unknown keep you from answering the call to go and tell, wherever God might lead. You'll find joy and hope in the unknown, as long as God is there.

Jesus said to them, "Do not be afraid. Go and tell my brothers to go to Galilee; there they will see me" (Matthew 28:10, NIV).

Don't be afraid. People are waiting to be told. Someone needs you to go and tell so that they might also see Jesus.

ANSWER THE CALL

- What's one thing you resisted trying or doing that you ended up loving? Why do we sometimes fight hardest against something for which we are best suited or called?

_____

_____

_____

_____

_____

- "Yes, but..." What conditions have you put on saying yes to God's call? Evaluate your reservations. What fear or issue is behind your hesitation or unwillingness in those areas?

_____

_____

_____

_____

_____

GO TELL!

Check out that thing or place you've been resisting. Read about the country or the program. Ask God to send just the right person across your path to make a connection. Ask God to make His will clear to you and your heart willing.

PRAY

Never Reached People Group: THE PASEMAH OF INDONESIA

Ask God to raise up intercessors with a heart for the Pasemah.

A Living Testimony

By *Josh Lovelace, Cambodia*

Theara's village now had a single believer with a story to tell.

God works to send His gospel message to never reached people groups, no matter how far away—or how close.

A young, unassuming girl named Theara came to Cambodia Bible Institute in Phnom Penh for ministerial training in 2015. She seemed shy and unsure of herself. However, her story opened our eyes to another side of Theara and reminded us of just how God works to send His gospel message to never reached people groups, no matter how far away—or how close.

Theara grew up in Kampong Cham Province, in a village with no Christian witness. Theara and her family viewed life from a Buddhist perspective intertwined with animistic practices. Their family struggled daily to make ends meet without any concept of Christ or His love for them.

When Theara was 17, her sister developed a mysterious illness. As good Buddhists, the family went to temple and made special offerings to earn good merit and a cure. But their efforts were in vain, and Theara's sister grew worse. Soon, she stood at the brink of death, and the family began to face the inevitable.

But a South Korean missionary heard about the situation while serving in a different area of Kampong Cham Province. The Holy Spirit spoke to him to go and pray for the sick girl. Neighbors pointed out the family's small house, curious as to why this man had come so far.

Upon arriving at the house, he asked the girl's parents for permission to pray for their sick daughter. Having exhausted their own efforts to find a cure, they were open to anyone offering hope. Entering the house, the missionary made his way to the dying girl's small bed. Keeping vigil beside the bed was Theara, filled with grief, as her sister was now very close to death. Quietly kneeling next to Theara, the missionary simply asked God to heal the sick girl in the name of Jesus Christ. Then he rose and left the house without fanfare, satisfied that he had completed the task the Lord had given him.

That simple, powerful prayer changed things. Within a few days, Theara's sister had completely recovered from her illness. But an even greater change had taken place in Theara. God moved in Theara's heart when she heard the missionary pray and intercede in Jesus' name. The rest of the villagers marveled and wondered how such a thing had come to be, but Theara knew that it had been the name of Jesus Christ. She believed. Her village now had a single believer with a story to tell about healing in Jesus' name.

Shortly after this miracle, Theara sought out a church in a different area of Kampong Cham Province, where she was discipled. During that time, it became obvious that she had a special gift—the gift of evangelism. In just two years, she led 50 people to Christ! The Lord was stirring her heart in two areas: a desire for ministry training and a call to return home to share the gospel in her village.

We saw Theara's special gift flourish during the two years she studied at our Bible school in Phnom Penh. She worked hard in the classroom and put her studies into practice every weekend when she returned to serve in Kampong Cham Province. I was privileged to have Theara in class for our Book of Acts course. She was always quiet but attentive as we studied the lives and ministries of the apostles. I could see the urgency of her call in her eyes and in her daily class work.

When I teach the Book of Acts, I ask students to name anywhere in the world they would like to go and minister. It's not uncommon for students to mention faraway places with well-known needs, such as Africa, to work with AIDS victims; India, to rescue young girls on the streets; or China, where the underground church needs strengthening. But Theara named a place I did not know. It was a remote place near her home village. I asked, "Theara, if you could go anywhere in the world, why would you choose that place?"

"It's near my village, and it has no gospel witness," she quietly replied. "That's why I want to go there."

In the Great Commission, Jesus sent His followers to evangelize all nations. But the real point was to tell those who most needed to hear. In Luke 8:38–39, a man Jesus had delivered wanted to follow Jesus to regions beyond. But Jesus had other plans:

Jesus sent him away, saying, "Return home and tell how much God has done for you." So the man went away and told all over town how much Jesus had done for him (Luke 8:38–39, NIV).

Theara is a living testimony of the Lord's grace to the people in her home province. She graduated from Cambodia Bible Institute in 2017 with an Associate of Arts degree in Bible and Church Ministries. She remains active in ministry in Kampong Cham Province and is reaching places that previously had no gospel witness. Her desire to go is stronger than ever and is fueled by urgency, just like the apostles in the Book of Acts.

ANSWER THE CALL

- As with the missionary's prayer for Theara's sister, every act of obedience to God impacts His kingdom in ways we can't imagine. What is God calling you to do today?

_____

_____

_____

_____

_____

- What unique connection do you have with a never reached people that God may be calling you to utilize?

_____

_____

_____

_____

_____

GO TELL!

You don't always have to go far to share the gospel with a never reached people group. Investigate avenues of reaching them in your local university or other community gathering spots.

PRAY

Never Reached People Group: CAMBODIA'S VIETNAMESE

Pray that God will raise up and empower believers to build a strong church to reach their own people.

GO IN

John 20:1-8 --------------------------------

*Now on the first day of the week Mary Magdalene came to the tomb early, while it was still dark, and saw that the stone had been taken away from the tomb. So she ran and went to Simon Peter and the other disciple, the one whom Jesus loved, and said to them, "They have taken the Lord out of the tomb, and we do not know where they have laid him." So Peter went out with the other disciple, and they were going toward the tomb. Both of them were running together, but the other disciple outran Peter and reached the tomb first. And stooping to look in, he saw the linen cloths lying there, **but he did not go in.** Then Simon Peter came, following him, and went into the tomb. He saw the linen cloths lying there, and the face cloth, which had been on Jesus' head, not lying with the linen cloths but folded up in a place by itself. Then the other disciple, who had reached the tomb first, **also went in, and he saw and believed;** (ESV)*

In and Out

By Greg Mundis, Executive Director, Assemblies of God World Missions

We only have a testimony if we have gone into the tomb ourselves.

There is a famous fast-food hamburger chain with restaurants scattered across the western United States called In-N-Out Burger. Their hamburgers, fries and shakes are delicious, and they pride themselves on good food and customer service. You're in and then quickly out and on your way.

In John 20:5–10, the disciples went into the tomb of Jesus, and after seeing it was empty, they quickly went out. For John and Peter, experiencing the empty tomb was life-changing. The mere act of going in was a step of faith.

Burial in Israel at that time was based upon the rich history and traditions in the Old Testament. Because of the climate and lack of knowledge of modern embalming methods, the dead were buried quickly. Some Old Testament figures were buried in the ground, but many were buried in caves. The tradition during Jesus' day was to wrap the body in linen cloths and cover it with myrrh and aloes. Joseph of Arimathea and Nicodemus initially performed this act of compassion and respect for Jesus.

At the time, people believed that the spirit of the dead person would hover over the body for three days after burial. It would then be an opportune time for the women to anoint Jesus and finish the burial wrapping. They expected to encounter a heavy stone with the seal of Rome over the opening of the sepulcher. Imagine their shock to see the stone rolled away! The Gospel of John describes Mary running to tell the apostles, and John and Peter immediately racing to the tomb.

Why was going into the tomb a step of faith? I believe faith was involved because they knew a tomb would have a Roman seal; they would be trespassing and possibly incur the wrath of Rome. However, civil law and the ramifications of going into the tomb paled in comparison to Peter's and then John's curiosity.

Also, remember the resurrection of Lazarus when Jesus was warned that the body had been in the tomb for four days? There would be an incredibly foul odor! So, to go into the tomb based on just Mary's words was an act of faith. It would be much like a child standing on the edge of a swimming pool with a parent in the water asking them to jump, promising to catch them. It takes faith to make a bold step into an arena that is unknown. Peter and John demonstrated this kind of faith by going into the tomb.

Peering in gives you an opinion; going in gives you a testimony.

Because they went in, they witnessed the miracle of the Resurrection. Despite their natural feelings of aversion and fear of disappointment, they went in. Because they went in, they became His witnesses.

How does this scene in John 20 apply to our lives? The first lesson that comes to mind is this: We must have faith to step into the unknown. Like John and Peter, do we? I really don't know why Peter bolted into the tomb while John looked in from the outside. Was Peter impulsive or full of faith—or both? Why did John hesitate? Did Peter's going into the tomb first give John courage? The Bible says that each of us has been given a measure of faith. To me, this is like each of us having muscles but not all of us exercising to perform at a maximum level. Is my faith dormant, or is it being exercised and growing?

When John and Peter walked out of the tomb, the Bible says that John saw and believed, but neither he nor Peter totally understood. Believing and understanding are like apples and oranges. I can say I believe in heaven, but I don't totally understand it. Our faith for acting is not in the how, what, when, or why, but in the who—Jesus, the Son of God. Be prepared to step into the tomb and come out believing in who Jesus is and what He wants you to do, even if you don't understand all that is involved.

The second lesson is that when you step into the unknown and see, you become a witness. You have a testimony. Revelation 12:11 says:

They triumphed over him by the blood of the Lamb and by the word of their testimony; they did not love their lives so much as to shrink from death (NIV).

One's testimony is a powerful weapon for righteousness and against the onslaught of the enemy. However, the testimony is only yours if you have gone into the tomb. Peering in gives you an opinion; going in gives you a testimony. In your walk of faith, each step is a building block in the testimony you can share. Don't just peer into what the prophetic faith passages of the Bible say. Go in, participate, and believe, and God will demonstrate His resurrection power in your life.

ANSWER THE CALL

- Are your faith muscles dormant or growing stronger? How can you exercise your faith more?

_____

_____

_____

_____

_____

- In what area is Jesus calling you to trust Him and jump in?

_____

_____

_____

_____

_____

GO IN!

Have you experienced Christ's resurrection power for yourself? Write out your testimony stemming from that encounter. Be prepared to share it when God opens a door.

PRAY

Never Reached People Group: THE MARANAO OF THE PHILIPPINES

Ask God to send more workers so that no Maranao man, woman, or child will remain never reached by the gospel.

Go In

By Cari Hurst

My children have always loved the water, more specifically the ocean. From the moment they could walk, they were either in a pool, or at a beach with one of us diligently by their side, exclaiming together, "Hi, sweetie! You can do it! Just jump right here! We're not going to let go of you! Just come on in, the water is so much fun!" With smiles in tow, they gladly obliged and experienced the refreshing sense of water covering their little bodies. At times, they swallowed a little more water than anticipated; but as long as they knew we were there, it was worth it, snotty noses and all. Those tiny tots are now a teen and tween, so gone are the days of jumping to "mommy and daddy." But they still have a fondness for the water, especially during the summer season. I can't help but think it all started by my husband encouraging them to simply *GO IN*.

The two [Peter and John] were running together; and the other disciple ran ahead faster than Peter and came to the tomb first; and stooping and looking in, he saw the linen wrappings lying there; but he did not go in. And so Simon Peter also came, following him, and entered the tomb; and he saw the linen wrappings lying there, and the face-cloth which had been on His head, not lying with the linen wrappings, but rolled up in a place by itself. So the other disciple who had first come to the tomb then also entered, and he saw and believed (John 20:4-8, NASB).

When we read this passage of Scripture from the Gospel of John, there are two people on the scene: Peter and John. What seems to be a race to see who could get to the tomb first, John clearly wins. Upon arrival, he hesitates. He saw the strips of linen where Jesus' body had been, but decided not to go inside. Wait, what? This is Jesus we're talking about. The One they had gladly given up everything for and decided to follow. And John, the beloved disciple, hesitated? Most versions clearly state, "he didn't *GO IN*." Simon Peter finally caught up with John and actually entered the tomb. Peter, the one in second place, went inside immediately, and then John followed. Finally, Scripture says, John goes inside.

I am baffled at his lack of urgency. After all, he was the first one there, but he hesitated. Then I stop and attempt to put myself in John's situation. This was Jesus, his teacher, Savior, and friend. Maybe he was overcome with grief. After seeing the remaining cloths where His body had been buried, it was just too much. Maybe he was waiting for Peter to catch up, because he knew this was something to grasp, but not alone. And then, it happened—he saw, not with his human eyes, but with the eyes of faith and believed.

Had my two tots not braved the water for the first time and "gotten in," they never would have known the joy of being in the water, cooling off on a hot summer day, putting on some goggles and searching for a pool toy or a certain kind of fish (in the ocean). So, here I sit and take a step back. Instead of pointing the finger at John and wondering *why* he waited to go inside, I forget the most important part—he did, and when he did everything changed.

What is keeping you from taking that first step? Jesus is calling and saying, "Just **GO IN**. I'm right here. I've got this." Instead, we choose to look at our immediate circumstances or maybe our own insecurities and convince ourselves to do everything BUT go in for what He is calling us to do. I'm sure the first disciples of Jesus experienced this. It is easy for us to assume they immediately followed and obeyed when He said, "Come." However, if we take the Gospels within context as a whole, we see a picture of various individuals with different abilities, job skills, and backgrounds who had an established relationship with Jesus the Messiah. Following Jesus is a commitment. A lifelong one.

Thirty years ago, I was a teenage girl who knew Jesus and knew church. One afternoon I was challenged with messages about an *intimate relationship with Jesus, knowing God and making Him known,* and then was sent off with my Bible, a notebook and pen, to hear what God was speaking. In that moment, under a giant tree in the hot Texas sun, everything changed. I could identify with John. I saw and believed. I experienced my *GO IN* moment. Since that time, I have been to nearly 50 nations, served as a missionary, pastored in a handful of states, along the way met my amazing husband of nearly 16 years, and had two amazing children (the teen and tween now). But without a doubt, the greatest title for me has been and will always be, follower of Jesus.

What are you waiting for? The greatest journey of your life awaits if you will simply take the next step. Jesus never guarantees us a carefree journey without its share of challenges along the way. Believe me, there are days where I feel there are more losses than gains (I have the scars to prove it!); but without a doubt, to GO IN is the most rewarding way to live!

ANSWER THE CALL

- Choose to be a follower of Jesus and have an unwavering commitment to Him.

_____

_____

_____

_____

_____

- Choose to drown out the voices and distractions around you and let the Holy Spirit guide you.

_____

_____

_____

_____

_____

GO IN!

What will going in look like in your life? Make a list of things causing you to hesitate and commit them to God in prayer. Ask the Holy Spirit to help you identify that first step you need to take. Then step in; in seeing, you will believe.

PRAY

Never Reached People Group: THE HAKKA CHINESE OF TAIWAN

Ask God to prepare the hearts of the Hakka Chinese for the coming of the gospel and prepare the hearts of workers to go and tell them.

Go in. See. Believe.

Hesitation is understandable so long as we don't let it paralyze us.

"The king is dead." When Thailand's beloved King Bhumibol Adulyadej died on October 13, 2016, the nation was plunged into a year of mourning. At the time, his impressive 70-year reign was the world's longest. His compassionate legacy benefited the Thai people on a daily basis, and they mourned as children grieving the loss of a beloved father. Color was stripped from everyday life, and seas of people in black wept. Memorials were raised in every province, restaurant and home. No joy was found in the Land of Smiles. I wept bitterly as a palpable blanket of sorrow covered this people and nation I love so dearly. My friends had lost their king, and with him, their hope.

Jesus was dead. Perhaps the disciples felt the same when the One they trusted to redeem Israel was crucified. Confused and afraid, they hid. Although the central theme of Jesus' teaching was His death and resurrection (Matthew 12:39–40; 16:21; John 2:18–22; 10:17–18), no one was inclined to look for the risen Lord. The full picture of God's redemptive plan for humanity remained hidden from the disciples. All their hopes lay buried with Jesus.

Upon hearing of the empty tomb, John outran Peter. He reached the tomb first, looked in, saw orderly linens, but hesitated to go in. When Peter caught up to John, he entered without hesitation. Then John went in and saw enough evidence to believe Jesus had risen.

When it comes to missions, each of us approaches the call to go in differently. Some of us hesitate to go in at all, lingering just outside. Uncertain of what awaits on the other side of obedience, we can't bring ourselves to enter this place of death—death to self, safety and comfort. "Maybe when the kids are grown...," we might say, or, "after I find a spouse." While I understand that the Lord gives each person special grace to endure and fulfill His call, some cannot bring themselves to say,

"Here I am. Send me!" (Isaiah 6:8, GW)

Missionary Isobel Kuhn said, "I believe that in each generation God has called enough men and women to evangelize all the yet unreached tribes of the earth. It is not God who does not call. It is man who will not respond!"

Nothing is accomplished by lingering at the entrance to the empty tomb. Hesitation is understandable so long as we don't let it paralyze us. John hesitated at first, but he didn't turn around and go home. Instead, he went in, saw the evidence, and was first to believe.

> **You are the one — the answer to someone's prayers.**

Likewise, others passionately jump into missions, only to arrive on the field and realize the cost was much greater than they anticipated. Peter's hesitation came when Jesus asked him three times, "Do you love me?" (John 21:15–17). In the original language, Jesus used the word *agape*, or "unconditional love." But Peter's response, "Yes, Lord; you know I love you," used the Greek word *phileo*, implying brotherly love or friendship.

How do we respond when Jesus asks us to go all in? With confidence in our commitment to Christ, we raise our hands, sing our songs, and declare our love and loyalty to Jesus until death on Sunday morning. Then Jesus presents an opportunity to go beyond praying or giving to leaving family and friends and investing our life on behalf of people yet to encounter the empty tomb. Our cornerstone comforts are threatened, and we hesitate. Surely Jesus isn't talking to me!

After His resurrection, Jesus drew an uncomfortable parallel between suffering and glory. In the road to Emmaus narrative, Jesus used the same *go in/enter in* word to describe His own purpose: "Was it not necessary that the Christ should suffer these things and enter into his glory?" (Luke 24:26 ESV). Suffering was the only way Jesus could redeem the world and reconcile humanity with His Father. Suffering preceded glory. Until Jesus returns to make all things new, the road to abundant life is a road of suffering.

Today's invitation to experience the empty tomb and risen Lord is the same as on Resurrection Sunday. *Go in. See. Believe.* Jesus calls us to go in wholeheartedly, without hesitation. All are commanded to participate in the Great Commission. No one who commits to following Jesus is allowed to skip out on obedience. Each of us has a role to play in God's mission to go, give, and pray for those who have not yet heard the good news.

How will you respond? Don't hesitate. Yes, sometimes we must follow blindly and crawl on broken roads of sorrow toward His glory, but He never leaves or forsakes us—not even for a moment. Not even when the king dies or the world crumbles hopelessly around us.

The revelation of the risen Lord brings the responsibility to go into all the world and preach the good news. If we don't, nations will perish for eternity. You are the one—the answer to someone's prayers. Don't hesitate. Trade the temporary comforts of this world for Christ's eternal glory. It'll be worth it. *Go in.*

"No reserves. No retreats. No regrets."—William Borden

ANSWER THE CALL

- Are you more like John or Peter? Explain. What makes you hesitate to embrace God's call to missions?

_____

_____

_____

_____

_____

- Are you responding to God's call with phileo or agape love? What does/will "entering in" to missions in full obedience to God look like in your life?

_____

_____

_____

_____

_____

GO IN!

Fold a piece of paper in half to create a balance sheet. On one half, list all of the things that are keeping you from fulfilling the Great Commission—weaknesses, obligations, fears, comforts, people, and stuff that you might have to give up. On the other, list the blessings of obedience. Be sure to include God's presence, provision, and eternal glory. Which outweighs the other?

PRAY

Never Reached People Group: THE ISAAN THAI

Ask God to arrange for Isaan Thai individuals to have divine appointments with Christ followers, wherever they may go.

Is Jesus Who He Says He Is?

By Mike and Missy Towers, Indonesia

Entering in gives birth to missions.

Imagine what the disciples likely experienced that first Easter. They had been living on a high with Jesus. There was talk of a kingdom where Jesus would reign. But then everything fell apart. Jesus was crucified, taking the disciples' hopes and dreams to the grave. Imagine the fear, grief and confusion. Jesus had promised so much, and now He was dead. Was it all a lie? Was Jesus who He'd said He was?

Just as hope seemed lost, they heard that the impossible had happened. Jesus had been raised from the dead. How could this be? Could John trust again? John was so excited to hear the news of an empty grave that he ran ahead of Peter. But something kept him from going in.

Stooping to look in, he saw the linen cloths lying there, but he did not go in (John 20:5, ESV).

Why did John hesitate? Perhaps he did not want to be disappointed. If Jesus was still in the grave, how could He be all He had claimed to be?

In 2016, my husband and I felt the Lord leading us to begin our family. But month after month, we dealt with the sting of negative pregnancy tests. Was something wrong? Had we misunderstood God? A year went by, and doubt found its home in my heart. My doctor told me that medical issues would make it extremely difficult to get pregnant. But what about God's leading and the promise He'd given me as a child that I'd be a mother?

We requested prayer. One night, as my husband and others laid hands on me, I felt God's presence in my physical body. A warmth came over me, specifically in my womb. I knew I had just received my miracle.

Six weeks later, I stared dumbfounded at the positive pregnancy test in my hand. Two days after that, I was on a plane to Indonesia with a team of Chi Alpha students for two weeks of ministry. As an added bonus, my husband and I had just been approved as missionary associates for a two-year term. Fear, excitement, anticipation and joy were just some of the emotions I felt.

But a few days into the trip, I began to feel unwell. Something felt off, and the symptoms that followed were more than worrisome. I soon realized I was miscarrying our miracle. Due to the early stage of the pregnancy and the lack of access to acceptable medical care, there was nothing I could do but pray. So, there I lay in a tiny hotel room, alone, on the other side of the world, as my miracle slowly slipped away.

Like John, I'd seen signs that resurrection power was at work, but I couldn't find the strength to step in.

Throughout the next few months, I struggled to understand why this happened. I was angry, confused, and I could feel depression settling over my heart. God had moved in such a powerful way; He had healed my body! He had given us this promise, so how could it not be true? Could I not trust it anymore? Could Jesus be who He says He is and still take this away from me?

I see myself during that time as John at the tomb's entrance. I'd experienced the miracles—I'd been pregnant—but it wasn't supposed to end this way. Like John, I'd seen signs that resurrection power was at work, but I couldn't find the strength to step in. I hesitated.

As John hesitated outside, Peter rushed past him into the tomb. When John finally followed him in, he saw and believed. Based on his newfound confidence in the living Christ, John would go on to be a leader in the newly formed church. A similar moment served to launch my own journey into missions. Only when we enter into God's presence and truly experience His glory for ourselves can we have the confidence to take His glory to the nations.

God is calling you to go into His presence, to see that His promises are true, and to believe. What fears are holding you back? What uncertainties? What hesitation?

I eventually moved past my hesitation and grief, allowing God to pour out His grace upon me. Part of my grieving process was coming to terms with the idea that I might not get pregnant again. I distinctly remember staying awake late one night talking with the Lord. I desperately wanted a child, but I felt peace, knowing that God had a more perfect plan and timeline. I knew God's faithfulness was real. And less than a week later, I discovered I was pregnant with my second child.

Through my loss, God gave me comfort and the assurance that, yes, He is indeed who He said He is. He is a good and faithful God. He gives and takes away, but what He gives is so much more than we can imagine. I now have a closeness with the Father that I don't believe would have been possible had it not been for our loss.

Now we're headed to the mission field as a family of three. We've walked through deep waters to experience the freshness of God's glory. We take that experience with us as we attempt to reach the people of Indonesia. Thank God for helping me overcome my hesitation to enter in. He is so faithful.

ANSWER THE CALL

- What circumstances have caused you to question God or His call on your life?

_____

_____

_____

_____

_____

- What is holding you back from entering in fully?

_____

_____

_____

_____

_____

GO IN!

Be honest with God about your questions, hurts and disappointments. Ask Him to give you courage to enter in to His presence and an empowering revelation of His glory. Then do what He tells you to do!

PRAY

Never Reached People Group: THE PAGAR ALAM OF INDONESIA

Ask God for a spiritual breakthrough among the Pagar Alam that would dispel centuries of spiritual darkness with the light of the gospel.

Let John Be John

By Jeff Hartensveld, Regional Director, Asia Pacific Missions

We can't rush the moment.

Peter and the other disciple started out for the tomb. They were both running, but the other disciple outran Peter and reached the tomb first. He stooped and looked in and saw the linen wrappings lying there, but he didn't go in. Then Simon Peter arrived and went inside. He also noticed the linen wrappings lying there, while the cloth that had covered Jesus' head was folded up and lying apart from the other wrappings. Then the disciple who had reached the tomb first also went in, and he saw and believed—for until then they still hadn't understood the Scriptures that said Jesus must rise from the dead (John 20:3–9, NLT).

What was that moment like when you first believed? In our tradition, many would point to a moment when they said the sinner's prayer or went forward in response to an altar call. But what caused you to say yes to Christ? There is a split second when, in the depths of our heart, we simply believe. This was what John experienced when he walked in and saw the grave, the cloth that had covered the face of the crucified Christ neatly folded off to the side. This had to be either the greatest setup of all time or the greatest miracle. In these verses, we see the moment when John believed and knew beyond a shadow of a doubt that Jesus Christ had risen.

Although John outran Peter, he hesitated to go all the way and enter the tomb. Some have speculated that John feared defiling himself by going near a dead body. It's also possible that the strong superstitions of the day made him afraid of the dead, or possibly a ghost. He did peek in, however, and he saw the abandoned grave wrappings.

Then Peter arrived, and he went headlong into the tomb with little pause for any of the thoughts that concerned John. Often, when it comes to believing, one person's courage can inspire someone else to follow and believe.

I wonder who you know that is on the edge of believing or going in? What's keeping them just outside? Is it a belief system that dictates what they should and shouldn't do? Or is it a fear of going against everything they've convinced themselves to be true? Are they possibly waiting for someone to lead them to take that final step of looking and seeing for themselves? Might that someone be you?

The truth is, no one is so different from Peter and John; the curious, the searching, the hesitant—they are our neighbors, our co-workers, our family members, and our old friends. They also live in distant lands with longing hearts that just won't be satisfied by anything other than an

...that moment of belief, is something that men and women around the world are still waiting to experience.

encounter with the risen Lord. They are waiting for someone to tell them about Jesus, who died on the cross for their sins and rose to live again.

John seemed to be the first person to put it all together and understand that Jesus had risen from the dead. That spark, that moment of belief, is something that men and women around the world are still waiting to experience. So, what will it take for a lot of such moments to take place? For starters, it's evident from this story that not everyone enters in the same way and at the same speed. Could we all agree that the Father in heaven wants all mankind to be saved and that each person is on a journey to see that happen?

We can't rush the moment. Let's not get upset with people who may be, like John, at the edge of believing but hesitate to go in. Many things in their lives could be causing such hesitation. Unfortunately, sometimes in our rush to see people saved, we push them into the tomb, only traumatizing them rather than preserving the harvest and letting them have that moment when they say, "I believe!"

Imagine if, instead, as John was peering into the tomb, Peter snuck up behind him and pushed him in, knowing that John was more thoughtful than he was and would need a push. A sacred moment would have been ruined forever had it happened that way. Peter went in as he did because he was Peter; John went in as he did because he was John. People from many tribes and tongues are waiting to go in, but many are just now peering in to get a better look.

Recently, I met a Muslim doctor who had treated a family member in the hospital. I asked him about his background, and when he found out that I was a minister, he told me, "I grew up near a church. I used to just get close to the windows and listen to the music and speaking because our tradition wouldn't let us go in."

Something—tradition, lack of knowledge, lack of opportunity— is keeping millions from going in and confronting the truth of the Resurrection. Will you pray with me for those who are still waiting to go in and believe for the first time?

ANSWER THE CALL

- What was it like when you first believed? How does remembering that encourage you to help others believe?

_____

_____

_____

_____

_____

- What are some ways in which we might be pushing people prematurely to make a decision for Christ? What can we do to slow down and help them to progress at their own pace?

_____

_____

_____

_____

_____

GO IN!

How can your courage inspire someone else to believe? Someone you encounter may need to hear your testimony. Ask God today to lead you to someone who needs you to show courage, go all in, and tell them.

PRAY

Never Reached People Group: THE AMBLONG OF VANUATU

Pray for a mighty move of the Spirit among the Amblong people that will open the hearts of many to Christ in your lifetime.

GO BEFORE

Mark 16:1-7 ------------------------------

When the Sabbath was past, Mary Magdalene, Mary the mother of James, and Salome bought spices, so that they might go and anoint him. And very early on the first day of the week, when the sun had risen, they went to the tomb. And they were saying to one another, "Who will roll away the stone for us from the entrance of the tomb?" And looking up, they saw that the stone had been rolled back—it was very large. And entering the tomb, they saw a young man sitting on the right side, dressed in a white robe, and they were alarmed. And he said to them, "Do not be alarmed. You seek Jesus of Nazareth, who was crucified. He has risen; he is not here. See the place where they laid him. But go, tell his disciples and Peter that he is going before you to Galilee. There you will see him, just as he told you." (ESV)

Our Struggle, His Strength

By Alan Johnson, Thailand

Failure, confusion, and spiritual blindness do not disqualify us from His service if we humble ourselves to let Jesus go before us and forgive, restore, and recommission us.

After the Lord's Supper, Jesus predicted His death and warned His disciples that they would be scattered. Then He told them:

"But after I have risen, I will go ahead of you into Galilee" (Matthew 26:32, Mark 14:28, NIV).

Jesus not only prepared His disciples for His death, but He promised there would be a future afterward. After His resurrection, Jesus told the women that He would go ahead of the disciples into Galilee (Matthew 28:7, Mark 16:7). His reiteration of this promise is theologically significant because it came after the disciples had denied Him and scattered at His arrest. When Jesus said that He would go before them and meet them, it brought the disciples hope of a fresh beginning and restoration. In His role as the Good Shepherd, Jesus went ahead of them, leading them to a place of forgiveness; reinstating and recommissioning them for their mission to the world.

Knowing the rest of the story, it's easy to forget how traumatic this time was for the disciples. They had been with Jesus for three years, observing and participating in His ministry. They had not comprehended Christ's predictions of His death and resurrection (Matthew 16:21; 20:17–19) or their own exalted positions in God's future rule (Matthew 19:28–30; Luke 22:29–30). Their overconfidence in themselves and in their commitment to Jesus (Mark 14:29–31; Luke 22:33–34; John 11:16), their flight at His arrest (Mark 14:50), and Peter's denial, followed by the Lord's cruel death, left them devastated. Luke captured this deep disappointment and crushed hope in the story of the risen Jesus joining the two disciples walking to Emmaus. Kept from recognizing Him, their faces were downcast. After recounting the recent events in Jerusalem, they concluded, "but we had hoped that he was the one who was going to redeem Israel" (Luke 24:21). On the evening of Resurrection Sunday, the disciples gathered together with doors locked for fear of the Jews (John 20:19).

Matthew captured the disorienting impact of this time with his observation that, as Jesus met them in Galilee, they worshiped Him, but some doubted (28:17). Scholars have puzzled over this, noting the incompatibility of worship and doubt.

Donald Hagner, in his commentary on Matthew in the *Word Biblical Commentary* series, argues that the key to understanding this passage lies in the meaning of the word *distaxein*, which is used only twice in the

> *It was not His resurrection they doubted, but their status with him...*

New Testament, both by Matthew (here and in 14:31). The word does not mean doubt or perplexity, but rather to be hesitant, indecisive, and uncertain. This fits well with Peter's situation in 14:31, where he stepped out into the water with Jesus, but started sinking when the wind frightened him. Jesus chided him for his lack of faith, not in the sense of doubting the ability of Jesus, but in the sense of his own inability to do what Jesus asked him to do by inviting him to walk to Him on the water.

Hagner noted that the Crucifixion would have left the disciples uncertain—unable to process all that was happening—even after Jesus appeared to them. It was not His resurrection they doubted, but their status with Him, what all of these events meant, and what might happen to them. Hagner calls the wavering between worship and indecision the struggle of every disciple. That's why Jesus' promise to always be with them was so critical.

Two important lessons stand out as we contemplate Jesus, who goes before us. The fact that Jesus goes before His people—that as the Good Shepherd He guides, directs and provides—reminds us that global mission is His doing, not ours. When we look at His promise to go before them to Galilee, we see how that moment is embedded in the disciples' journey with Jesus. It's a path marked by success and failure, by confusion and misunderstanding, by experiences that reveal their pettiness and selfish ambition, their spiritual dullness, and their captivity to their world's system of status and honor. It's a path that ends in failure and abandoning the One in whom they'd placed all their hopes. But Jesus went before them, regathered them, forgave and healed them, and made them His emissaries to the world.

Remarkably, Jesus is pleased to use people like us to accomplish His mission. Failure, confusion, and spiritual blindness do not disqualify us from His service if we humble ourselves to let Jesus go before us and forgive, restore, and recommission us.

Another lesson in the scenario of Jesus going before us, sending the disciples back to Galilee to meet Him, followed by His ascension, the coming of the Spirit, the initial proclamation, and then persecution reminds us that there is process and delay. Jesus' mission, which is global in scope, is not a straightforward line where we can expect only victory after victory until our final goal is reached. There is no naïve triumphalism in Jesus' going before us; the nations do not bow at His feet simply because we show up. Jesus goes before us to promise His authority and presence to the end of the age. *When* that end arrives is not our concern; we go forth with His promises that give us hope in dark and discouraging days and that assure us of His purposes being accomplished.

ANSWER THE CALL

- Even Jesus' closest, most effective co-workers and friends failed Him and needed to be restored and recommissioned. What hope does that give to imperfect people like us?

_____

_____

_____

_____

_____

- Why is it important to be reminded that global missions is God's doing and not ours? How can we balance that truth with our responsibility to obey and follow Jesus' call to global evangelism?

_____

_____

_____

_____

_____

GO BEFORE!

Confusion and doubt often come just before a fresh revelation of the risen Lord. Be honest with the Lord. Tell Him what you don't understand and your own weaknesses and failures as you've tried to follow Him. Trust Him—and thank Him—for going before you, even when you can't see or feel Him near you.

PRAY

Never Reached People Group: ETHNIC THAI BUDDHISTS

Pray for miracles, signs and wonders among the ethnic Thai Buddhists that will point them to our powerful God who loves them.

Gone Before

The fruit we see is because Jesus has gone before us.

While itinerating at a small church, I showed a picture of the remote mountainous area to which God was leading us. As I explained our call to share the gospel with those who had never heard the name of Jesus, tears streamed down the wrinkled face of an elderly Asian man there. I spoke about the underground church, which has continued to grow in the midst of intense persecution, and asked listeners to pray for a powerful move of God among the never reached people of this region.

Curious, I went to talk with the emotional Asian grandfather after concluding. As his son translated, the man excitedly explained that the photos I had shown were of his home village. The province where God was sending us was where he had been born and lived for 30 years before, fleeing war, he had brought his young family to America.

Through tears, he told me of his intercession for the people of his homeland: For more than 40 years, he'd pled with God to send someone to the mountains to share the good news of Christ with the family and friends he'd left behind. He desperately wanted them to know Jesus. He said, "Today my prayers have been answered, because you and your family are going!"

As I left that divine appointment, he was still weeping and thanking me repeatedly for answering the call of God; our Heavenly Father whispered two truths to my spirit:

1. I will never send you where I haven't gone before you.

As the angel said to Mary:

"Go, tell his disciples and Peter. 'He is going ahead of you into Galilee'" (Mark 16:7, NIV).

I'll be honest, my faith had been seriously wavering. My heart was anxious about the overwhelming task to which God was calling us. My wife and I were launching out with our young son into a Third World, communist country. We didn't know the language, we'd never set foot in the place He had called us to live, and we only knew two people in the entire country—and they lived eight hours away down a mountain road. We had allowed our eyes to focus on the obstacles and difficulties ahead rather than on the One who had gone before us to provide everything we'd need.

Were there unknowns at every turn as we prepared to move to Southeast Asia? Absolutely! Could we physically see how Jesus was there ahead of us and preparing everything for us there? No, we couldn't. We first had to step out of the safety of home and into the unknown of

----
*Our prayers for
never reached
people around
the world matter.*

His calling. We had to trust Him to be faithful to His promise, "There you will see him, just as he told you" (Mark 16:7).

When we finally arrived in our Southeast Asian nation home, could we see that Jesus was already there? Absolutely! Did we find a house? Yes, the exact house we needed. Because Jesus was there. Did we have electricity and water every day? Well, no...but Jesus was there. Did we almost lose our minds learning a new tonal language? Definitely! And Jesus was there.

Did God provide relationships with neighbors, friends and ministry partners? Yes! Because Jesus was there. Did we see people come to know the one true and living God? A resounding yes! Because Jesus was there. Have all the difficulties been worth it? Absolutely! Because Jesus is still here.

2. Through relentless prayer, we join Jesus in going before and move God's hand on behalf of the never reached.

As Gabriel told Daniel (Daniel 9:23), "As soon as you began to pray, a word went out." As soon as that grandfather started praying, heaven began to move to usher God's Kingdom into those mountains. Our prayers for never reached people around the world matter. When we intercede for the lost, we join Jesus where He is already at work, pushing back the darkness in every never reached place across the globe. Through intercession, we join Him in clearing the way through the wilderness, making a straight path through the wasteland, and smoothing out the rough places so the glory of God may be revealed in every nation and among every tribe (Isaiah 40:3–5).

The fruit we see is because Jesus has gone before us. Today, we are tasting the fruit of a grandfather's prayers. We have found favor with a communist government because people are praying, and Jesus continues to go before us. Bible studies and discipleship classes have begun because Jesus is pushing back the darkness all around us. It matters that we join Jesus in the "going before" through intercession. The eternities of people around the world hang in the balance.

My Asian friend has worked for his own people from 10,000 miles away. Are you willing to join Jesus in the "going before" by interceding for those who have never heard the gospel? Will you be the answer to those prayers by going to a never reached people, trusting Jesus to always go before you? As heaven moves and Jesus goes before us, we will see a tremendous harvest among the never reached in Asia and around the world.

ANSWER THE CALL

- What evidence have you seen in your own life of God's going before you?

_____

_____

_____

_____

_____

- Will you commit to interceding on behalf of a never reached people group, asking Jesus to go before the gospel message, preparing the way?

_____

_____

_____

_____

GO BEFORE!

Spend time in prayer every day this week, asking God to give you a burden for never reached people and allowing the Holy Spirit to pray through you for specific needs.

PRAY

Never Reached People Group: THE KHMER (SOUTH) OF VIETNAM

Pray for believers at work among the Khmer, that they and their families may have wisdom, courage, stamina, provision, favor, protection and grace as ambassadors of Christ's love.

Already There

I want you in this. I'm going before you. I'll be there when you get there.

The sun cast shadows on the pavement at my feet. I could feel the heat through my sandals as beads of sweat slid from my forehead to my nose. My child Rose's shoes slapped quickly against the sidewalk between shrieks of delight at each exotic discovery in our new neighborhood. The unfamiliar road stretched out before us, and I wondered about my family's future. Did we belong here? Could we do this on our own?

Peter. I always come back to Peter. I see in him so much of myself. Not the rock on which Jesus said He would build the Church, but the stumbling stone Peter showed himself to be before Jesus' death and resurrection. I hope that someday I'll be more like Jesus, but if I'm honest, today I'm Peter.

Peter was passionate and spontaneous. You never knew what he would say or do. One minute he was jumping out of the boat to join Jesus for a stroll on the water, and the next he needed Jesus to save him from drowning. In a matter of a few hours, he chopped off a man's ear to defend Jesus, and then denied he even knew Him. The reality is that Peter messed up...a lot. He made grand gestures, took bold steps, and spoke big words, but he choked, he sank, and he failed. When things got hot, his tongue betrayed his heart. When the pressure was on, he ran.

But have you noticed this beautiful small detail? When the women arrived at Jesus' tomb to anoint His body, an angel told them:

"You are looking for Jesus the Nazarene, who was crucified. He has risen! He is not here. See the place where they laid him. But go, tell his disciples and Peter, 'He is going ahead of you into Galilee. There you will see him, just as he told you" *(Mark 16:6,7, NIV).*

Why did the angel mention Peter separately? Why wasn't Peter with his closest friends when they would need comfort most? My theory is that he was hiding because he was ashamed; I would have been. At the moment of truth, Peter had failed Jesus in the very way he had just bragged he never would. Can anyone relate? I can. I talk big—I have big, well-intentioned plans, which usually means that my missteps and shortcomings are more epic, and, because of my big proclamations, even more shameful.

What's amazing, but not at all surprising, is that Jesus knew Peter would be hiding. He sent a Peter-specific message via the angel. "Tell the disciples that I'm going ahead of them, that I want to be with them...and don't forget to tell Peter. Please tell Peter that I'll meet him there, too." That's just like Jesus. He didn't discount Peter, and that's the first thing Jesus wanted him to know. Peter didn't have to be afraid to face Jesus. He reassured Peter

> *If you look in the mirror and find tragic flaws, you're in good company.*

with a message: "I want you in this. I'm going before you. I'll be there when you get there."

A missionary often walks hand in hand with uncertainty. What will it be like living in this foreign context? Will I be able to learn the language? Will I be able to find cheese? But the hardest questions I've asked as a missionary are those I've asked of myself. Am I cut out for this? Am I holy enough? Am I going to mess this thing up? As a Peter personality, these questions are particularly hard for me. I know my shortcomings all too well. The wonderful truth is that Jesus does too, and He still lets me follow Him around, learn His ways, and reach the world for Him. Jesus has gone before me into my foreign home, but He has also gone before as pertains to myself. He sees my personality, with all its twists and turns, its darkest depths and unfortunate shallows, and still sees fit to call me to this life.

Jesus knew Peter was passionate: On one hand, that passion drew a man's blood; on the other, it drew crowds to hear his testimony. If you look in the mirror and find tragic flaws, you're in good company. The same Peter who denied Jesus became a strong, early voice of the New Testament church. Jesus knows who you are. He knew you before you knew you, and He has called you in spite of, and often because of, that. Why? Like Peter, you may be a stumbling block with potential to be a foundational rock.

We often go into never reached parts of the world with the idea that we are carrying Jesus with us, but my experience is much like Peter's. In all my feelings of inadequacy, when I'm in over my head and feel like running away, Jesus reminds me that I'm not taking Him anywhere. He's already there.

My gaze followed the moss slowly up the walls of ancient buildings so unlike anything from home. Feeling small, I tightened my grip on the leather straps of my backpack and tucked my elbows in tight. This place wasn't foreign; I was. I raised my hand to my brow, blocking the glare, and somehow, through the sunlight, I saw Him—Jesus. He had gone before us. He had met us here.

ANSWER THE CALL

- In what ways are you like or unlike Peter? What previous failures are making you ashamed and want to hide?

_____

_____

_____

_____

_____

- How does Jesus' message to Peter encourage you in light of your own failures? What can it teach us about compassion for others' failings?

_____

_____

_____

_____

_____

GO BEFORE!

Let go of your past failures—the missed opportunities, times you said no, half-hearted attempts, and outright rebellion—and heed Jesus' message to meet Him again. Ask Him to forgive you, change you, and even use your failures for His glory. Then trust that He is going before you in whatever endeavor to which He calls you.

PRAY

Never Reached People Group: THE JAVA PESISIR LOR OF INDONESIA

Ask God to reveal himself to the Java Pesisir Lor people through dreams and visions.

He Has Been Waiting for You

By Sam Paris, Vanuatu

As soon as he'd heard we'd entered his village, he knew that we were the men in his dream.

> *...I heard the Holy Spirit whisper, "One more hill."*

Hot season was at its peak. Sweat ran down my back, dripped down my legs, and pooled in my shoes. When I reached my hand around to touch the back of my backpack, I could feel it was drenched. I had sweated through the entire contents of my backpack and out the other side. It had been days since I'd slept on a mattress. The smell of campfire smoke was thick in my hair, and my skin had a thick covering of sweat mingled with the ash constantly falling from an erupting volcano. It made a weird muddy lotion on my skin that felt slimy.

Four days before, I'd set out from my village on the west side of the island of Tanna. My goal was to go to areas I'd never been and make contact with remote tribes in hopes of establishing relationships and sharing the gospel. The communities I hoped to visit have no access to a church and little contact with outsiders. There are no roads to these villages, only muddy vine-covered trails up coastal mountains and into deep valleys.

After three days of hard work, exciting encounters, and exhaustion, local pastor David Iao and I were finally heading home, praising God for success on our mission. God had gone before us and prepared the way. We'd just had to show up, share His love, and watch Him do the rest. I was already sweating before we even set out on the trail early on the fourth morning. My plan was to get down the trail as quickly as possible, be back to my truck by midday, and be home by evening. There, I'd enjoy a hot meal while telling my family about what God had done. I was about to find out that God was not yet finished.

The journey down the mountain took all morning, as we stopped in every village we encountered. Shortly after lunch, we passed through a valley and hopped stones across a river. On the other side, I recognized the well-traveled trail that would connect to the main road. To our left was a small trail that seemed to go straight up the mountain before angling off into a cluster of coconut trees and disappearing into the jungle. We turned to start down the main trail, knowing that if we pushed it, we could still make it home by dinner.

That's when I heard the Holy Spirit whisper, "One more hill." I stopped, looked at the small trail to the left, and told Pastor Iao that I felt that we were supposed to follow it. He agreed, and, in spite of my whole body longing to be clean and my back aching to stretch out on my bed— not to mention seeing my beautiful wife and kids—we started back up the mountain.

One more hill turned into an afternoon of climbing. At times it was so steep we had to climb with our hands. Several hours later, just when I was beginning to think the trail didn't go any farther, we broke through the jungle and came upon a small village. Just then, someone called out, "They are here! They are here!"

Some people were sitting in the middle of the village, so we approached and shook their hands. As we did, a young man stood up and said, "He has been waiting for you." Then, without any explanation, he turned and walked away, indicating that we should follow.

He led us to a small hut and disappeared inside. I took off my shoes and followed him in. As my eyes adjusted to the dark, I saw white eyes looking back at me. Seated on a mat next to the young man was a village elder whose hair and beard were as white as his eyes. I could tell he was blind— and had been for a long time. The elder's legs were stretched out in front of him; on one of his shins, I could see bone sticking through the skin, which had closed around the bone. I could see that the bone had been filed down long ago so that the bone was now smooth.

The old man began to talk. With tears, he told us of his dream the previous night, in which God had told him, "Two men who belong to Me will come to your hut tomorrow." As soon as he'd heard we'd entered the village, he knew that we were the men in his dream. Then he told us that, when he was young, he had fallen off a cliff, cried out to God as he was falling, and lived. Since that time, he had promised God that when he met a man who belonged to God, he would give him land for building a church.

"I want you to build a church here," he told us. "I want my village to know God!" I was overwhelmed by God's awesomeness. He had gone before us! When God calls you, He goes before you. He is just waiting for us to go.

ANSWER THE CALL

- What promptings of the Holy Spirit have you followed? What was the result?

_____

_____

_____

_____

_____

- Think back: Have you missed promptings in the busyness and noise of daily life, your uncertainty, or reluctance to be inconvenienced or play the fool? What opportunity may have been squandered?

_____

_____

_____

_____

_____

GO BEFORE!

Today, as you go about your tasks, listen for the still, small voice of the Holy Spirit. Don't question or try to rationalize it away. Follow His leading! He is going before you, preparing the way.

PRAY

Never Reached People Group: THE MIDDLE BUSH PEOPLE OF VANUATU

Ask God to raise up intercessors with a heart for Vanuatu's Middle Bush People.

Follow the Father

By Jonathan Lowrance, Japan

He has not asked us to go anywhere He himself has not been first.

"Go quickly and tell his disciples: 'He has risen from the dead and is going ahead of you into Galilee. There you will see him'" *(Matthew 28:7, NIV).*

...it's who goes before us that matters most.

An array of incredible sights, sounds, and smells assaulted my senses as we walked out of the Tokyo train station. We were instantly swallowed by a sea of people, unseen currents swiftly moving everyone toward some unknown destination. As we came to a crosswalk aptly named "Scramble" in Japanese, a large dam in the flow of workers formed as people on every side of the intersection patiently waited for the light to turn green. As we came to an abrupt halt, I glanced at my 4-year-old daughter beside me. Her tiny hand firmly in mine, she waited with confidence, knowing her father was leading the way. She trusted that I knew the destination and how to get there safely. In a beautiful expression of innocence, her sole focus was to simply *follow the father*. What a perfect analogy of how our Heavenly Father goes before us, guiding us on a journey that seemingly always tests our faith. But no matter what may come against us, it's who goes before us that matters most.

When I read through the accounts of Jesus' life, I'm often struck by the fact that He was always two steps ahead of His followers. I see two distinct benefits in this. First, as the disciples learned they could trust His leadership, their faith developed into a powerful fear-killing force. History's tyrants have led through fear and intimidation, but Jesus led like a great father. This not only taught them to *believe* in the miraculous, but the building of their faith enabled them to *do* the miraculous. This leads to the second benefit—the disciples could clearly see their own path by following Jesus' example. Following in Jesus' footsteps, the disciples healed the sick, cast out demons, preached the gospel, and showed compassion for those around them.

Jesus said, "Whoever believes in me will do the works I have been doing, and they will do even greater things than these, because I am going to the Father" (John 14:12). Just as I desire for my child Rose's abilities to surpass my own, Jesus wanted His followers to do even greater things. Jesus' words imply that greater things would not and could not happen if He did not go before them to the Father.

At times, I've found myself veering from God's intended route, as if to say, "It's OK, God, I can take it from here." Given the benefits of God's go-before-us modus operandi, why would we risk the harm of stepping off the path He has blazed for us? By neglecting our daily communication with the Holy Spirit, we may lose sight of the One we follow. This can lead to frustration and battles He simply hasn't asked us to fight.

Just as the angel sent trustworthy messengers to direct Jesus' disciples, God often sends people into our lives with a needed word of direction. Before our first missionary term in Japan, I was eating dinner with the pastor of a large church after speaking in their service. I was full of passion for the never reached in Japan and excitement for the next season of our lives. At the same time, I was uncertain about the particular area of ministry God was leading us toward. I'd spent a lot of time in prayer without receiving a clear direction from the Holy Spirit. The pastor encouraged my wife and me to work in our areas of strength. It didn't seem particularly significant at the time, but the Holy Spirit continued to bring this advice to my mind countless times. I finally began to listen to what God was saying to me. That insignificant word turned out to be the catalyst for what would become our primary ministry direction in Japan. God is always leading. Are we always listening?

Sometimes, in spite of our earnestness to follow God, we lose sight of the path in front of us. Not knowing where to go next can be scary and confusing. But God remembers your human limitations. He will not leave you stranded. Deuteronomy 31:8 says, "The Lord himself goes before you and will be with you; he will never leave you nor forsake you. Do not be afraid; do not be discouraged." We can put aside our fears and reservations because, when God goes before us, we are confident He already knows our path and destination. He will not lead us astray.

What does this mean for us as His children? We can have the reassurance and peace of knowing that He has not asked us to go anywhere that He himself has not been first. Your past, present and future are all laid bare to Him. He knows every route, difficulty and danger you might face. You're not lost in the dark without a hand to hold. Rather, you're following God's very sure and purposeful footsteps, which are leading you to a destination He has gloriously designed and chosen you for. God is in complete control, and He goes before you. Hold tightly to His promises, and simply follow the Father.

ANSWER THE CALL

- What step of faith is God leading you to take?

  _____

  _____

  _____

  _____

  _____

- What examples of His faithfulness in your previous circumstances and areas of ministry have given you confidence that He will take your hand and go before you?

  _____

  _____

  _____

  _____

  _____

GO BEFORE!

Look back at your life and ministry and trace the evidence of God's leading you, preparing the way before you, and preparing you. With this clearer picture in mind, where might the trajectory of God's leading take you next? Are you ready to say yes and step out in faith?

PRAY

Never Reached People Group: THE JAPANESE

Pray that God will raise up and empower believers from Japan to build a strong church to reach their own people.

GO TOGETHER

John 21:1-3 ---------------------------------

*After this Jesus revealed himself again to the disciples by the Sea of Tiberias, and he revealed himself in this way. Simon Peter, Thomas (called the Twin), Nathanael of Cana in Galilee, the sons of Zebedee, and two others of his disciples were together. Simon Peter said to them, "I am going fishing." They said to him, "**We will go with you.**" They went out and got into the boat, but that night they caught nothing.* (ESV)

Go With God

By Chris Carter, Japan

We are never Lone Rangers.

From its inception, our mission required unity and teamwork.

For Christians, there are no lone rangers. Jesus did not issue the Great Commission to His followers in isolation. The women came to the empty tomb together and were sent to the disciples together. The disciples encountered Jesus together, hearing Jesus' call and instructions together. The church waited for the Holy Spirit and received empowerment together. From its inception, our mission required unity and teamwork.

The communal nature of our Christian calling to go and tell jumps off the pages of the New Testament. Paul traveled and worked with teams. Many of Paul's epistles were authored in team fashion. For instance, Paul and Sosthenes collaborated on 1 Corinthians, and Paul, Silas, and Timothy are named as authors of 1 Thessalonians. The church received its marching orders together, and it largely obeyed together.

Clearly, teamwork seems to be the New Testament ideal for Christians, but those of us on the mission field know that reality often falls short of the ideal. Personality conflicts often split teams, and missionaries regularly list their own colleagues when enumerating difficulties of missionary life. Remember Paul and Barnabas' partnership-ending disagreement over John Mark? Beyond interpersonal dysfunction, sometimes obedience itself leaves us alone and isolated in the task of missions. Countless modern missionaries have found themselves cut off from other believers in the dark and dangerous lands of their calling. Paul too found himself alone in Athens when persecution in Thessalonica separated him from his team. Just before his execution at the hands of Nero, Paul wrote: "At my first defense, no one came to my support, but everyone deserted me" (2 Timothy 4:16, NIV).

Yet even when Paul had to labor without help and companionship, he was not alone. Even after stating that everyone had deserted him, in his next breath the apostle wrote:

"But the Lord stood at my side and gave me strength, so that through me the message might be fully proclaimed and all the Gentiles might hear it" (2 Timothy 4:17, NIV).

At all times, Paul remained cognizant of being God's co-worker. Even if we are alone, we are never lone rangers.

Most of us can recite Matthew 28:19–20 by heart. But we often omit the last sentence of verse 20: "Behold, I am with you always, to the end of the age" (Matthew 28:20, ESV). This sentence begins with the Greek word ἰδοὺ, the imperative form of the verb *to look*. Although the NIV literal translation might be "pay attention!"

Next, Jesus said: "I am with you." This takes us back to Matthew 1:23: The virgin will conceive and give birth to a son, and they will call him Immanuel (which means 'God with us')". It also reminds us of Jesus' prophetic words about the church in Matthew 18: "Where two or three gather in my name, there am I with them" (Matthew 18:20). Matthew—beginning, middle and end—concerns the fulfillment of Isaiah's prophecy about Immanuel. Jesus' birth, life, death and resurrection lead to one concluding statement about a new and permanent state of affairs: "I am with you." This underlies the mission of the church. This is no solitary mission but one for the whole community; thus, Jesus used the plural *you* (ὑμῶν). He promised to be with *all* who respond to His commission.

Going together means going with God. The next words load the concept with heavy theological weight and importance. After promising to accompany us, Jesus defined the limits of missions with the words: "to the very end of the age" (Matthew 28:20). The word *end* (συντελείας) always speaks of the Second Coming—the day when Jesus will return and gather His church. On that day, He'll also judge the world. From the moment the church received its marching orders, Jesus stressed the link between the mission of the church and His return. When we complete the task, the end of the age will come. He will come, and we will be with Him. All opportunity for repentance will end.

Going with God means that the agenda is His, not ours. If we went only by ourselves or even only with each other, we would likely have this-worldly notions about success. We might be deluded into thinking our purpose rests in building megachurches. Or we might be seduced into supposing that success lies in the strength of our organization or the beauty of our buildings. But going with God transposes everything into an otherworldly key. Success cannot be measured by the standards of this world. The twists and turns of persecution and freedom, poverty and riches, and sympathetic and unsympathetic societies have no relevance. Instead, everything comes down to the day of His coming. Will we belong to Him on that day? Will the nations belong to Him on that day through our obedience? Or will we only have the keys to a crumbling earthly kingdom to hand over to our Lord on that day? Have we gone with Him, or have we gone by ourselves?

ANSWER THE CALL

- What do you count as your greatest successes? Do your successes line up with how the world judges success or how God does?

_____

_____

_____

_____

_____

- If today were the day of Christ's second coming, what would you have to show for your life?

_____

_____

_____

_____

_____

GO TOGETHER!

Read Matthew's Gospel, tracing evidence of Christ going with His followers. Then evaluate your own life. When have you seen affirmations of God's presence?

PRAY

Never Reached People Group: THE BANJAR OF INDONESIA

Ask God to send more workers so that no Banjar man, woman or child will remain never reached by the gospel.

Holding Bloody Ridge—Together

By Bryan Webb, Area Director, Pacific Oceania

Together we can change the destiny of nations.

Simon Peter said to them, "I am going fishing." They said to him, "We will go with you" (John 21:3, ESV).

Going together—it's what Christians do. In this passage, we see the disciples after a roller-coaster ride of emotions. On the journey to Jerusalem the preceding Palm Sunday, they had argued about who would be greatest in Christ's kingdom. When Jesus told them to untie the donkey and her colt and bring them to Him, their expectations rose. They knew Zechariah's prophecy of Israel's king riding on a colt. This was it! The coronation was imminent! Surprisingly, Jesus wandered Jerusalem a bit and went home. What a letdown. Surely, He would assert His authority soon.

Instead, Jesus criticized political and religious leaders. The week ended with His arrest and crucifixion. Dismay, confusion, hopelessness and grief filled the disciples' hearts. Their emotions crashed to an ultimate low.

Then, early Sunday morning, Mary came from the tomb saying Jesus was alive, and Jesus appeared to the disciples later. Grief changed to delirious joy. Their dashed hopes were reborn. Acts 1:6 records them even daring once again to broach the subject of when Jesus would establish His (their) kingdom.

But then came days when they didn't know where Jesus was—blank spots, like pages missing from a book. John 20:26 records that eight days passed between the first time Jesus appeared to the disciples and the second time. Then more days passed. Peter, suffering from emotional whiplash, gave in to discouragement.

Have you faced the blank pages? They occasionally come when following Christ—days when God seems silent. On such days, we need each other most.

"I am going fishing," Peter said, throwing in the towel by announcing his intention to return to the family business. He was through hoping for a Kingdom position; just give him something safe, dependable and predictable—like fishing. Rather than criticizing Peter for giving up, the disciples responded in a way that set the tone for generations of Christians to follow: "We will go with you."

Christians go together. *That's why we gather for worship.* We can worship at home or at the lake, but we gather together for the benefit of others—for the one needing prayer, encouragement, or a warm hug from a fellow believer. Alone we meet with God, but together we strengthen each other. *That's why we give to the church.* We realize we are called to do some things that are too big for us alone. If we go together, our tithes and offerings accomplish ministry in our world that far exceeds our personal capacity. *It's why Christians work together in missions.* Alone, it's impossible; we must go together.

In World War II, the Japanese war machine rolled across the Pacific. It swept aside every force it faced—until the U.S. Marines landed on the island of Guadalcanal on August 7, 1942. They captured what would be known as Henderson Field and took the high ground above the airport.

The battle of Bloody Ridge followed. Outnumbered 10 to 1 and short on food and ammunition, the Marines were ordered to hold the ridge above Henderson Field. Today, Bloody Ridge is just a grassy knoll, although the foxholes remain. When I recently visited Bloody Ridge, I stood in the last foxhole.

Going inland from the coast, Bloody Ridge narrows to a sharp point. The ground then slopes into a low saddle before rising toward the mountains. This saddle presented the best opportunity for the Japanese force to advance. Two men manned that last foxhole with a .50 caliber machine gun. Their assignment? Create an impenetrable wall of lead across the saddle, denying the attacking force access to Henderson Field.

Early in the fight, a Japanese soldier lobbed a grenade into the foxhole. It exploded, blinding one Marine and severing the thumb of the second. For five hours, unrelieved, those two Marines held their position together, the blinded man firing the machine gun with the maimed man directing his fire. Alone, neither man was capable of completing the mission, but together, they changed the course of the battle, turned the tide of war, and changed the history of nations.

None of us can fulfill Christ's mission alone, but together we can change the destiny of nations. What must we all do together if our mission is to succeed?

We must pray together. Missionaries planting the church among never reached people face unprecedented spiritual resistance. Strongholds will be broken down only through the church's collective prayers.

We must give. To fulfill the mission, some must go, others must give to send them. In Romans 10, Paul addresses the need for some to go preach to those who haven't heard. Bluntly he asks, "How are they to preach unless they are sent?" (Romans 10:15, ESV). Going together means sitting down with your checkbook and allowing the Holy Spirit to direct your missions giving.

We must go. I've been told repeatedly, "I'm so glad God called you to go over there. I don't think I could do it." As if God has given me a greater responsibility than them. As if my family is called to make greater sacrifices for this mission. The truth is, we share equally in the obligation of the Great Commission. We give, not to bless a missionary or to ease our conscience, but because by giving, we go together.

ANSWER THE CALL

- What gifts, skills or resources has God given you to use for Him? Are you making the most of everything He has given you—including opportunities?

  _____

  _____

  _____

- When you endure blank-page days—when God seems silent—how do you respond? Do you wait, persevere, or go fishing? What might be the purpose of such days?

  _____

  _____

  _____

- What can you do to encourage someone going through a time of blank pages?

  _____

  _____

  _____

GO TOGETHER!

Prayerfully, make a plan to maximize the gifts, resources and opportunities God has given you to use for Him. How can you improve the effectiveness of your praying, giving, doing and going?

PRAY

Never Reached People Group: THE MAGINDANO OF THE PHILIPPINES

Ask God to prepare the hearts of the Magindano for the coming of the gospel and the hearts of workers to go and tell them.

Not the Dream Team

We expected our ministry partners would look like us and think like us.

After a year of language school, my family and I launched out to a remote mountain province in Southeast Asia to see how the Father might lead us in engaging never reached people groups there. We had already experienced that blind leap of faith in coming to this country, yet this move left us feeling like we were floundering in the dark. God had given us a passion to see a thriving ministry birthed that would impact the entire province and daily communicate the gospel in creative ways, since open evangelism isn't allowed here. We knew we had to obey and go, but we also felt deeply alone. We were launching out into a place of great spiritual darkness.

We knew that the Father sends His people out together, yet we were going alone. Still, we believed the Father would be faithful. We took the plunge, trusting Him to provide everything we would need to pioneer this work and make His name known in this Buddhist country. We knew that He would bring ministry partners alongside us.

Subconsciously, we expected those ministry partners to look like us, think like us, have U.S. passports, and speak English. I think we even expected them to love Chick-fil-A and sweet tea as much as we did! Little did we know, God was bringing together an even better team, including Mai, a pastor from the local underground church who didn't speak English.

Although Mai's life started in the chaos of the Vietnam War, God guided and protected her. Thirty years later, although it was illegal to own any Christian material, a missionary risked his life to give her a Bible. She read it in three months, but it was three years before she fully understood and believed. In the following years, she led secret prayer meetings with the only other believers in the entire province. From a tiny group of five, God built a thriving underground church. Twenty years later, Mai serves as a pastor of more than 100 people.

We have been challenged by Mai's bold faith in sharing the gospel. She taught us how, even in this closed country, we could boldly share Jesus. Despite the language barrier, we partnered to bring healthcare and scholarships to poor families. We prayed together for students, leaders, teachers and doctors. As we joined together in prayer and ministry, we saw monsoons stop so we could travel dangerous mountain roads, dying infants recover, and people receive Christ throughout the province.

As God continued to bind our family with Mai in life and ministry, there were certainly challenges along the way. The direct communication style of Western culture conflicts with the circular communication here. Once, when local government officials were being especially difficult,

> *From time to time, we'll have to clear out the mess created by going together.*

we felt like pushing back against their unreasonable demands. Mai calmed us down and taught us the culturally appropriate response. We first built a relationship with them, and then scheduled another meeting to resolve the conflict. By listening to the ministry partner God had given us, the conflict was resolved, and we have walked in unprecedented favor with our local government leaders.

If God had built the team we wanted the way we wanted it to be built, it's likely we would not have been allowed to continue working in this country. We needed our local teammate, and we needed to learn to work together.

As Proverbs 14:4 (NLT) says, "Without oxen a stable stays clean, but you need a strong ox for a large harvest." Together, we are believing for a massive harvest among never reached people groups around us. From time to time, we'll have to clear out the mess created by going together. But we must humble ourselves, learn from the ministry partners God has brought to us, and clean out that stable. It will be worth it because the harvest is more than worth it.

As the new day was dawning, Mary Magdalene and the other Mary went out to visit the tomb (Matthew 28:1).

God joined together an unlikely group of people in Mary and the other women who went to the tomb that morning. They included the sister of Jesus' mother, a woman who had been delivered from seven demons, and the wife of one of Herod's officials (Luke 8:3; 24:10). God joined them together in discipleship, they went together to the tomb, and together, they experienced the greatest miracle of all time!

As we eagerly engage never reached people across Asia Pacific, we trust the Father to knit us together with ministry partners *He* chooses. We commit to not be consumed with building a team of our choosing but willingly humble ourselves and be sanctified through the process of living life together.

God has continued to grow our unlikely team. We daily launch out in what feels like the deep darkness of this population of animists and Buddhists with fewer than 2 percent Christians. We believe that, someday, the truth of the Resurrection will sweep across this nation. Together, we faithfully believe that we are going to see the dawn of salvation come to these never reached peoples. And then we will run back, like Mary and the other women did, to you, the faithful disciples, and say, "Come see! Resurrection power has come to this place!"

ANSWER THE CALL

- What are your weaknesses where you need someone else to be strong?

_____

_____

_____

_____

_____

- Examine your own biases and assumptions. Who might you be rejecting or overlooking that God has perfectly fitted for your team?

_____

_____

_____

_____

_____

GO TOGETHER!

Almost every human fault or weakness is the flip side of a gift or strength (stubbornness and determination, for instance). When a co-worker or associate annoys you, or their habits or way of thinking conflict with yours, consider what strength that represents that you might be overlooking. Find the strength, and you'll see what God might see in them.

PRAY

Never Reached People Group: THE LAO PONG

Ask God to arrange for Lao Pong individuals to have divine appointments with Christ followers, wherever they may go.

Faithful Women

By Greg Mundis, Executive Director, Assemblies of God World Missions

When women answer the call to go together, the gates of hell must tremble.

I talked with a youth pastor once who said he'd done a thorough study of the word *go*. He'd studied the Hebrew, Aramaic and Greek, digging deep into its meaning. He looked at the etymology and root meaning and came to a startling conclusion—the word *go* means go!

Going involves a choice, a choice that every person must make. *Go* could mean going across one's house to an unbelieving family member, or it could mean going overseas to reach lost people. When one hears God's divine call to go overseas, it means making an individual choice. Notice that the choice to go is not restricted to one's economic position, intelligence level, or gender. There is, however, a choice of going alone or going together.

Matthew 28:1 says, "Mary Magdalene and the other Mary went to look at the tomb." Matthew 28:8 says they "hurried away from the tomb, afraid yet filled with joy, and ran to tell his disciples" (NIV).

First, although Jesus was unjustly labeled a criminal, the women remained faithful to Him. The capacity of women to demonstrate trust, faith, and faithfulness is highlighted in the Gospels. Consider Luke 8, where the women followed Jesus and His disciples to minister to them. This lifestyle was not easy. These women endured difficult conditions as they served Jesus. As I think about what I admire about Assemblies of God World Missions and our rich history, women's service in missions tops my list.

I think of Alice Wood, who in 1910 went to Argentina and shared the gospel; her first furlough was in 1960! Talk about faithful! I think about Alice Luce, who in 1921 said, "When we go forth to preach the Full Gospel, are we going to expect an experience like that of the denominational missionaries, or shall we look for signs to follow?"[1] Wow! Alice, like so many of our female missionaries, not only heard and responded yes to the call to go, but she also went in the power of the Holy Spirit. One final example is Anna Tomasek. In 1936, she opened an orphanage on the Nepal-India border. "Her compassion for suffering and abandoned children became an outreach that resulted in the planting of the church in Nepal."[2] Today, Nepal has hundreds of churches and thousands of believers.

Second, pioneer women missionaries accomplished incredible exploits for the Kingdom. We are deeply grateful for their contribution. And, as in the case of the two Marys, teams of women made amazing

[1] *Marvels & Miracles, Assemblies of God World Missions*, 2014, p. 24.
[2] *Ibid.*, p. 27.

> *The significance of going together cannot be underestimated.*

contributions to the work of the Kingdom. Consider the example of Pauline Smith and Adeline Wichman. In 1946, immediately after World War II, they arrived in Ghana, Africa, where they planted churches, taught Bible school, translated literature, evangelized, and ministered. Consider this excerpt from their newsletter: "We experienced the thrill of having the whole village of Mimmima turn to Christ in one day. The inhabitants of the village gathered together, destroyed their fetishes, and tore down the gateposts to the houses dedicated to their gods."[3]

When women answer the call to go together, the gates of hell must tremble. The significance of going together cannot be underestimated. Ecclesiastes says, "Two are better than one, because they have a good return for their labor: If either of them falls down, one can help the other up. But pity anyone who falls and has no one to help them up....Though one may be overpowered, two can defend themselves. A cord of three strands is not quickly broken" (4:9–12).

AGWM owes much to the ministry of women. They have contributed enormously to our mission and our missiology. What lessons can we learn from the Bible and our history? First, as the Bible says, God is no respecter of persons. Indeed, this is seen in the biblical context, historically, and in the present day. Remember Joel's prophecy, quoted by Peter:

"In the last days, God says, I will pour out my Spirit on all people. Your sons and daughters will prophesy, your young men will see visions, your old men will dream dreams. Even on my servants, both men and women, I will pour out my Spirit in those days, and they will prophesy....And everyone who calls on the name of the Lord will be saved" (Acts 2:17–21, NIV).

Those the Holy Spirit calls into ministry, He equips, enables and empowers, no matter who they are. Women are a powerful reservoir and resource for God to use. God has given them sensitivity to the Spirit, intuition, endurance, tenacity, faith and faithfulness. We rejoice over the Spirit of God's calling and empowering of women in missions work.

If you're a woman, and the Lord is speaking to your heart, don't miss the opportunity He is giving you. Rebuke the negative thoughts; rebuke the stereotyping of men; rebuke the enemy who would attack you with fear, as he did Mary Magdalene and the other Mary. Remember, although they felt fear, there was joy—joy unspeakable and full of glory. This is the joy of the Lord that is our strength. Respond positively to God's leading, and you'll discover a joyful adventure in serving Him in missions.

[3] *Ibid., p. 29.*

ANSWER THE CALL

- What are some unique and essential gifts women bring to missions?

  _____

  _____

  _____

- What woman or women have been most inspiring and influential in your Christian walk and missions involvement? Describe their impact.

  _____

  _____

  _____

- What evidence have you seen of the complementary nature of men and women in missions?

  _____

  _____

  _____

GO TOGETHER!

If you're a woman, consider how you can make associations with other women or resources that will allow you to reach your full potential for God and open doors for involvement in missions. If you're a man, consider ways you can maximize your ministry by fully involving both women and men.

PRAY

Never Reached People Group: MYANMAR'S SHAN

Ask God for a spiritual breakthrough among the Shan that would dispel centuries of spiritual darkness with the light of the gospel.

Giants

By Brandon Powell, Thailand

We have the honor and privilege of standing on the shoulders of giants who have gone before us.

I think back to moments like the evening services at the youth retreats and conventions, with the speaker calling out for young people to open themselves to be baptized in the Holy Spirit and embrace God's unique calling for us individually. I internalized the call as something specific that God wanted to do through me rather than what I would get to do with God through the community of believers. I'm incredibly thankful for the men and women who put countless hours into these experiences for me to have that special, unique encounter with God. My life has been forever changed because of the sacrifices that were made to cultivate an atmosphere conducive to being used by God. Millennials like me crave authenticity, especially in our faith communities. The good news—for all generations of believers—is this: We *can* live out our unique callings in an authentic community, but we must be intentional about it.

Through dark seasons my wife and I have experienced, we've come to realize the importance of being *together* in a community. Inside each human is a blueprint configured differently for each of us. But we're wired similarly, because we share the same Creator. That Creator has instilled in us a deep desire to belong and live together. The moment we look to gain prominence, seeking to be greater than another, we step out of God's design for our life—and that's a scary place to be. One of the most effective ways that we can proactively die to this impulse and give our all for the kingdom of God in community is to be cognizant of others around us. We must seek to honor others and build them up, working in harmony with others instead of trying to do it alone. We can start by honoring the people who have gone before us.

Since we are surrounded by such a great cloud of witnesses, let us throw off everything that hinders and the sin that so easily entangles. And let us run with perseverance the race marked out for us (Hebrews 12:1, NIV).

Hebrews 11 and 12 paint a vivid picture for us of a great cloud of witnesses—heroes of the faith. I'm incredibly thankful for the missionaries who have done the hard work before me, breaking the hard soil and building a foundation upon which I can build. Regardless of the type of work you find yourself doing, we all have the honor and privilege of standing on the shoulders of giants who went before us.

> *God intended for us to serve together.*

Equally important are the people with whom we are serving. This can include your spouse, teammates from your organization, or your church. From the very beginning, God intended for us to serve together. As a general rule of thumb, when possible, go together. The people we serve with can often be the best and the most difficult parts of life. In fact, trouble with co-workers is a common reason missionaries leave the mission field. But serving together is also one of the most vital parts of our faith, and it calls for us to honor and encourage each other (John 13:35). Community is a gift from God. We must embrace, nurture, protect and treasure our fellowship with others.

Of course, our most vital partnership is with the Holy Spirit. So often we proclaim that we're working *for* God. But this infers that God isn't involved in the process. How terrifying that would be! We have the honor of serving *with* the Holy Spirit. God is not absent from this work of restoring all mankind to himself. He is present and longs to accomplish this work *with* us. Moses, one of these great witnesses surrounding us today, was wise enough to plead with God, "If your Presence does not go with us, do not send us up from here" (Exodus 33:15). He recognized that he didn't stand a chance without God, and he was so close to God that he didn't *want* to go without Him. May we have that same heart for God and a desire to go *with* Him.

If you, like many Millennials today, find yourself struggling to make a decision about how to live your calling, consider your motivations. If you've put the brakes on an opportunity, why is that? Is it because God has told you to wait, or because you are waiting for a better opportunity? As I had to remind myself, while you wait, countless people from never reached people groups are dying. If you feel called to missions, I implore you to pick one of these groups and join the battle for souls. And, if no one is there yet, which is still possible today, take someone with you!

ANSWER THE CALL

- What evidence do you see in your own life of God's call to work together?

_____

_____

_____

_____

_____

- Whose shoulders have you stood upon to reach this place in your life or mission? Who paved the way for your achievements?

_____

_____

_____

_____

_____

GO TOGETHER!

Write a letter thanking some of the "giants" whose shoulders you've stood upon. Tell them how they've impacted your life or ministry. You just might be the encouragement they need to keep them going strong.

Find a way to encourage or mentor a younger Christian, encouraging them to find their place in the Great Commission. Pray for them daily and share your wisdom and experience with them.

PRAY

Never Reached People Group: THAILAND'S SOUTHERN BURMESE

Pray for a mighty move of the Spirit among the Southern Burmese people that will open the hearts of many to Christ in your lifetime.

GO FURTHER

Luke 24:28-35 ----------------------------

*So they drew near to the village to which they were going. **He acted as if he were going farther**, but they urged him strongly, saying, "Stay with us, for it is toward evening and the day is now far spent." So he went in to stay with them. When he was at table with them, he took the bread and blessed and broke it and gave it to them. And their eyes were opened, and they recognized him. And he vanished from their sight. They said to each other, "Did not our hearts burn within us while he talked to us on the road, while he opened to us the Scriptures?" And they rose that same hour and returned to Jerusalem. And they found the eleven and those who were with them gathered together, saying, "The Lord has risen indeed, and has appeared to Simon!" Then they told what had happened on the road, and how he was known to them in the breaking of the bread. (ESV)*

Beyond Naguragum

By Bryan Webb, Area Director, Pacific Oceania

The Spirit of Christ always propels us to go further.

They drew near to the village to which they were going. He acted as if he were going farther (Luke 24:28, ESV).

As a new missionary to Vanuatu, I followed a local church leader 25 miles into the interior of Espiritu Santo to visit a fledgling church planted among a never reached tribe. Early in the morning, we left our truck at Unguru and began the trek up the Ora River. Slowly, the path petered out. Walking midstream, we entered a slot canyon; massive granite walls rose above us, their sides marked intermittently by cascading waterfalls. It was indescribably beautiful.

Clouds gathered above us, and torrential rain forced us to hide in riverside caves. Previously clear, the Ora turned angry red as the rain swelled its banks. Twenty-eight times we swam the Ora. By day's end, I was stumbling over boulders, exhausted by my backpack's weight and the river's force. At sundown, we entered a tiny village. The chief welcomed us into his hut. His wives, bare breasted and with bones through their noses, spread banana leaves on the dirt floor for our bed and boiled a slimy soup of island cabbage.

After an impromptu evangelistic service, I collapsed onto the banana-leaf bed. Early the next morning, I rose, aching more than I ever had in my life, pulled on my still-wet socks and boots, strapped on my backpack, and we set out.

Within the first hour, we encountered a 765-foot waterfall. The path, steep and narrow with dizzying drop-offs on each side, led up the razor-sharp ridge beside the waterfall. There were no trees, and the early morning sun beat down relentlessly. A third of the way up, my legs began to tremble. Halfway up, I was gasping for breath. By the time I neared the top of the ridge, black spots floated in front of my eyes, and I felt precariously close to passing out.

Near the top of the waterfall, a tree grew horizontally out of the cliff face, stretching out over the abyss. I dropped my backpack, took one last desperate swig at my empty water bottle, and collapsed onto the tree. I stretched out full length on the trunk, oblivious to the danger of the empty space beneath me. "This is it," I told my trail mates. "I can go no further."

They tried to encourage me, telling me of a clear cold spring just ahead and assuring me that the worst was behind me. They promised that Naguragum was just a bit further, but I was done. I was completely beyond my endurance and training. One of my friends dug in his bag to find some dried meat, another brought out a bit of candy, and another ran ahead to fill his canteen at the spring. I ate, drank, rested, and reluctantly moved on.

The climb was nearly over, the spring was clear, cold, and delicious. Naguragum was not, however, just a bit further. Once I reached the spring, I dove into its clear water, drank deeply, and slowly felt my strength returning.

I stood at the base of a pristine alpine valley. A gurgling stream split it down the middle. The walls of the valley were covered in flowering trees. It was breathtakingly beautiful. A friend pointed to a hill high above the valley, it was topped with a massive nabanga tree. "See that tree?" he asked. "That's Naguragum."

I noticed a thick tangle of jagged mountain peaks dark beyond Naguragum. "What about there?" I pointed. "Are there villages there? What is it like to go there?" Chief Norman, our guide, shook his head. "No, missionary, all those who go there sell their lives. It's much worse than this."

Standing in the cold spring water, exhausted by the climb and totally spent, I had no doubt I would climb those peaks and preach the gospel to their villages. The Spirit of Christ always propels us to go further. It's His nature.

When Jesus met with two disciples on the road to Emmaus, they were heartbroken and perplexed. They knew the prophecies regarding Messiah, yet they were confused, primarily because they were interpreting them from an egocentric, nationalistic perspective.

As Jesus walked with them, He explained from the Scriptures why it was necessary for Messiah to suffer and be raised from the dead. He moved the focus off of them and onto himself. When they reached their stopping place, He acted as if He were going further.

Why? Because that's what He does; that's His nature. When Christ called His disciples, He found Peter and Andrew; going a little further, He found James and John. While the disciples napped in the Garden of Gethsemane, Jesus, going a little further, prayed.

All of us reach our stopping place. Maybe it's a matter of physical exhaustion, sickness, or reaching an emotional breaking point. Some stop because they've gone as far as their faith can see. Maybe, like the disciples, you've stopped because this is as far as you intended to go. Too often, we reach our stopping place because our focus is on ourselves or our circumstances rather than Christ.

Notice that Christ didn't condemn the disciples for stopping. At their insistence, He turned aside, entered the house, and broke bread with them, before opening their eyes so that they recognized Him. The impact of His revelation propelled the disciples to also go further. Instead of spending the night in Emmaus, they rushed back to Jerusalem with the good news.

Earlier they had insisted, "It is toward evening and the day is now far spent" (verse 29). Yet when Christ revealed himself, they immediately began the seven-mile journey back to Jerusalem. The best part? While they were there discussing the events with the other disciples, Christ appeared to them. When they went further, they discovered Christ was already there.

ANSWER THE CALL

- What would going further mean for you? What stops you?

_____

_____

_____

_____

_____

- Where would you dare to go if you were confident Christ would be there waiting for you?

_____

_____

_____

_____

_____

GO FURTHER!

Prayerfully determine what going one step further would look like in your Christian walk and mission and take it—today.

PRAY

Never Reached People Group: THE NABANGALAS OF VANUATU

Ask God to reveal himself to the Nabangalas people through dreams and visions.

Eight More

By Cari Hurst

You can go further.

"Eight more." I'm still challenged by those words every time I work out. Let me explain. Six years ago, I decided to do my first early morning boot camp class. For some reason, I chose the middle of winter—in Chicagoland, no less! I vividly remember one of those early morning drives when the thermometer on my car registered below zero, reminding me just how frigid it really was. On that particular morning, I removed my warm layers and moved slowly from one station to the next. Each time I thought I had done my best, my boot camp instructor pushed me a little bit further. "Eight more," she pressed me. "I know you can do just eight more. Even if you think you've done all you can, you always have at least eight more repetitions left inside you if you'll try." As much as I hated to admit it, she was absolutely right.

In this Christian life, we often want to throw in the towel and give up. But the Lord is right there with us saying, "Eight more. I know you can do it. There's more to you than you think. I'm right here, and I want to do this with you. You just have to let Me. Together we can go further!"

After His resurrection, Jesus inspired two discouraged disciples to give Him "eight more." On the seven-mile road from Jerusalem—where Jesus was crucified—to Emmaus, Jesus drew near to the two men. They didn't realize their new traveling companion was their Lord. The Bible says, "God prevented them from recognizing him" (Luke 24:16, TPT). The last thing they knew for certain was that Jesus, the One they had followed and loved, was dead. They seemed confused by a report traveling around that His body wasn't in the tomb where He was buried. In fact, some women had reported encountering angels who told them that Jesus was alive. I love how The Passion Translation phrases Jesus' response: "Why are you so thick-headed? Why do you find it so hard to believe every word the prophets have spoken?" (Luke 24:25). But Jesus didn't just chide them for their lack of understanding; He went further: "Beginning with Moses and all the Prophets, he interpreted to them in all the Scriptures the things concerning himself" (Luke 24:27, ESV).

When the two reached their destination, Jesus acted as if He were going further. But they pleaded with Him to stay with them—it was too late to go any further. Jesus not only stayed with the disciples; He revealed himself to them.

> *He's calling you to go further in this moment, to deepen your commitment to Him.*

He went in to stay with them. When He had reclined at the table with them, He took the bread and blessed it, and breaking it, He began giving it to them. Then their eyes were opened and they recognized Him; and He vanished from their sight (Luke 24:29–31, NASB).

Suddenly energized, it no longer seemed too late for traveling; the two got back on the road that same hour and returned to Jerusalem to tell the others—Jesus is alive! So often in life, what's important isn't where you're going but who you're going with. The crucial part of the disciples' journey that day wasn't their destination but who they encountered and that He opened their eyes. Jesus helped them see that God was using even the difficulties and suffering for His eternal purposes. In their brief time together, Jesus awakened their burning hearts (sounds like a workout to me) to the truth about himself and what He was calling them to do.

How often we get wrapped up in our destination instead of focusing on our divine traveling companion. *I wish I were there instead of here, we think. If I could just get there, God would use me.* But God wants to use you right here, right now. He's calling you to go further in this moment, to deepen your commitment to Him.

What's your "eight more"? Where are the areas of your life where you have settled for just enough, though you know in your heart you have more to give? A beautiful part of this story is that Jesus was with them the entire time. Even when they didn't recognize Him, He was still there.

Here are some life lessons I've learned along the way:

- When we go further, He's always there, no matter where we are on our journey.

- When we go further, it not only deepens our commitment to Christ, but reflects Him to everyone we meet.

- When we go further, we know we can keep going even when we fall, fail, and don't have anything left. We can go further in His strength, not our own.

ANSWER THE CALL

- What's making your heart burn today as Christ reveals himself and His plan for you?

_____

_____

_____

_____

_____

- What "eight more" is God pressing you to do—to keep going for just a little longer, a little more?

_____

_____

_____

_____

_____

GO FURTHER!

When you're weary, discouraged, or adrift, press on. When you don't understand why things have turned out this way and can't see the path forward, don't give up. Persevere. Give God "eight more." Not only do you have more within you than you imagined, your eyes might be on the verge of being opened. You can do it—eight more!

PRAY

Never Reached People Group: THE KANGEAN OF INDONESIA

Pray for believers at work among the Kangean, that they and their families may have wisdom, courage, stamina, provision, favor, protection and grace as ambassadors of Christ's love.

Beyond the Clubhouse

By Dan Betzer, Pastor, First Assembly of God, Fort Myers, Florida

Our church can go further when we recognize the risen Lord.

I am particularly drawn to the drama of two of Jesus' followers trudging home to Emmaus after the Crucifixion. Suddenly they were joined by Jesus, whom they could not immediately recognize. While the disciples believed that they had arrived at their destination (Luke 24:28), Jesus would have continued on, going further. When they, wanting more of Him, urged Him to remain with them, He did stay, but only until He revealed himself to them.

Let's make this very practical: I'm a pastor, and I have been for well over half a century. Early in my ministry, I knew virtually nothing about missions. I didn't really understand my pastoral role in the Great Commission, regarding either my personal involvement or my responsibility to lead the congregation to follow Christ's command. Our church was small, with an average attendance of 80–100. We had a cute little chapel, but we couldn't pay the bills. Our annual church budget was $16,000 for everything—mortgage, salary, utilities—everything.

Notice that I didn't mention missions. That's because we didn't give to missions. We had no money for that. We only needed a little more than $300 a week in tithes and offerings to meet our budget, but we were *not* getting $300 a week—or even close. How could we have supported missionaries? Soon we had racked up a general fund deficit of thousands of dollars.

Churches and families that cut missions when their budgets get tight find that their financial crises worsen. That's because they're cutting or diminishing the very thing God honors. We aren't called to stop; we're called to go further. I desperately cried out to God, "Why don't You help us?" I felt in my spirit His response, "Dan, I'm not helping you because you're not in the same business I am. You are in the church business, but I'm in the redemption business. When you get involved in My business—taking My gospel to the waiting world—I'll take care of your church business."

That was a shock to me and our little board. Were we truly not being obedient to God? Precisely! We were not. We really were not much more than a glorified civic club, using God's house as our clubhouse.

In response to God's prompting, we immediately scheduled a full missionary convention, a practice I still follow. Our little congregation began to seek God, asking forgiveness for having set aside the most important thing of all—obedience to His command. It is truly miraculous—supernatural—what begins to happen when our hearts burn within us and we beg Christ to be with us when He wants to go further.

> *We give, go, and pray because Jesus told us to.*

What a great theme for a missions convention—Going Further!

By the end of our first convention, our missions offering was $32,000—remarkable, for a little church that couldn't come up with $300 a week to pay the bills! So, what happened to the general fund? It immediately doubled. In six months, it had doubled again...and then again. We began buying property for expansion—with cash, not loans. Within one year, the church had grown to well over 300.

Please understand: We don't give to get. We give, go, and pray because Jesus told us to. We take care of His interest, His world view...and He takes care of us. It's just as simple as that.

My teacher, the legendary Dr. Oswald J. Smith (the founder of the 20th century missions faith promise movement, the man Billy Graham said was the greatest influence on his life) pounded into me, "Dan, God will never owe you money! If you can't go to the mission field personally, then you must send a substitute!"

Every believer must have a world view and a resolve to go further. John 3:16 makes it clear: God so loved *the world*. Jesus commanded, "Go into all *the world*." Before returning to heaven, Jesus gave us the reason for the infilling of the Holy Spirit:

"Ye shall receive power, after that the Holy Ghost is come upon you: and ye shall be witnesses unto me both in Jerusalem, and in all Judaea, and in Samaria, and unto the uttermost part of the earth" (Acts 1:8, KJV).

Many believers will protest, "Well, we're reaching our town for the Lord." Hopefully, that's true, but go further! Set your sights on Judea, Samaria and uttermost part of the earth.

After half a century of pursuing missions with a passion in our church, I can say to you: Every miracle of provision of supply in the church I have witnessed has been a direct or indirect response to our obedience to God's command to go into all the world.

Pastors and church leaders often come to my study to inquire why the church is so blessed, why thousands attend, and why money never seems to be a great challenge. I always respond with one word: *Missions!* That comes first. We currently support 535 missionaries on a monthly basis—and have never missed one month. It's a supernatural supply, believe me. Folks have started coming to the church who tell me, "Pastor, we have been looking for a congregation that is not just building pretty sanctuaries and always thinking about themselves." These folks share our commitment to reaching the lost by obeying the Great Commission. There's no other reason for our growth and stability. It's *Missions!*

ANSWER THE CALL

- What does your giving to missions say about your commitment to obeying the Great Commission?

_____

_____

_____

_____

_____

- What can you do to go further with missions than ever before?

_____

_____

_____

_____

_____

GO FURTHER!

Take stock of where you are right now as far as fulfilling the Great Commission. What would going further look like for you? Ask God to open your eyes and make your heart burn for the lost.

PRAY

Never Reached People Group: THE IRANUN OF PHILIPPINES

Pray for miracles, signs, and wonders among the Iranun that will point them to our powerful God who loves them.

Rose's Awakening

By Katie Benson, Indonesia

She became a new creation, and then she went further.

Imagine going your entire life hearing about Jesus but not knowing Him. Imagine thinking the priest was the only one who could really know God. Imagine believing your sins were only forgiven once a year when you kissed the feet of a statue of Jesus and having to carry the weight of your sins the rest of the year. That's what it was like for Rose, a young girl from a never reached people group of 3.4 million in South Sumatra.

When Rose and Dina, her best friend, walked into Chi Alpha for the first time, they were just excited to get to practice their English with native speakers. Both girls were in my small group, and I immediately saw potential in them. I made a goal of discipling the girls. After a few dinners and hangouts, we formed a weekly Bible study. I asked each girl to share her story. Dina spoke of a past similar to mine—of being engaged, breaking off the engagement, and coming to understand the love of Christ. Rose said that although she was Catholic, she didn't really care about religion. She was angry and bitter. Her mother had recently died, and her father had not handled the situation well. Rose doubted God and wondered why a God who loved her would allow such a terrible thing to happen.

Still, Rose agreed to meet to study the Bible. Basically, Rose wanted to please Dina, one of her closest friends. Dina typically took over conversations, and Rose simply nodded in agreement. I wanted to meet with Rose one on one to hear her thoughts, but Rose avoided being alone with me. Frustrated, I prayed a bold prayer. "God, make it so Dina cannot come to Bible study this week." Dina had a flat tire and couldn't make it, so Rose said she wouldn't be coming either. But I urged her to come, and for some reason, she agreed to do so.

That night, we discussed what it meant to find our identity in Christ. Looking puzzled, she asked, "How can anyone find their identity in Christ if they have to go to the priest to pray and have their sins forgiven?" I began to share the Romans Road, a simple plan of salvation, and she began to question all that she knew. She was amazed that I could ask for forgiveness of my sins at any time. She began to understand that I had an intimate relationship with Jesus. With tears in her eyes, she said, "But, Katie, why would Christ die for me? Look at me! I've made so many mistakes. This could not be for me."

"That's exactly why you need Him," I replied. Suddenly, throwing the papers in her hands into the air, she raised her hands, and shouted, "I want this! I want to know Jesus. I want to really know Him!"

Now Rose leads a small group and tells unbelievers about Jesus.

That night, Rose committed to going further and knowing Christ in a personal way. She later said of that Bible study, "I didn't want to come, but something told me I had to go. I'm glad I listened. My life is changed."

God wanted her to go even further, but Rose was hesitant. When Dina asked me about water baptism, Rose thought the idea was crazy. She had been sprinkled in water as a baby, and she made it clear that she was not interested in going further. Rose just sat and observed as Dina and I talked and studied what the Bible said about water baptism. But when we finished, Rose said, "I need this. I want to go further. I want to publicly declare that I know Jesus."

When Rose was baptized, she was immediately touched by the Holy Spirit. She wanted more.

At the next Bible study, Rose asked again about the Holy Spirit. "I want to experience that again."

"You can," I replied. "Every day." When we started to worship, she was filled with joy and couldn't stop laughing and crying. She wanted to go still further. She developed intimacy with the Lord, experiencing healing and forgiveness within her family. She no longer walked in anger but in grace. She became a new creation. And still she went further.

There's so much more. Let's get on with it! (Hebrews 6:3, MSG).

We invited Rose to join the leadership team. She initially said no, feeling inadequate. But when we encouraged her to pray about the invitation, she soon agreed. Now Rose leads a small group and tells unbelievers about Jesus. Rose hangs out with girls to build trust and create relationships where she can share Christ. Rose has taken it further; no longer content just to know Christ, she makes Him known to others. She has been completely changed, and she shares her good news wherever she goes.

In spite of Rose's amazing progress, she's not satisfied. She knows there is still more, and she wants to grow. In all she does, Rose looks for opportunities to take her faith further. God has more in store for Rose, for she is willing to go further.

ANSWER THE CALL

- Who do you know who is resisting God that you believe God wants to take further?

_____

_____

_____

_____

_____

- How can you intentionally invest in his or her life today?

_____

_____

_____

_____

_____

GO FURTHER!

Step out boldly in faith for another brother or sister in Christ. After praying about it, tell them of the promise and opportunity you see for them and challenge them to go further with God to fulfill that potential and God's call on their lives.

PRAY

Never Reached People Group: THE DAMPELAS OF INDONESIA

Ask God to raise up intercessors with a heart for the Dampelas.

Still More

By Mark Lehmann, Pastor, Cornerstone Church, Bowie, Maryland

No matter how much we think we know or have experienced, there is more.

"While it is good that we seek to know the Holy One, it is probably not so good to presume that we ever complete the task." —Dietrich Bonhoeffer

In one of my favorite Bible passages, on the Road to Emmaus, Jesus intersects the lives of two of His followers who had given up and were headed in the wrong direction. This encounter will reveal to them and us the compelling call to go further with the Lord. Although they had witnessed the Crucifixion and heard the women's report of the empty tomb, it seemed like nonsense to them. These disciples left Jerusalem discouraged and disappointed by what had happened. Worse yet, they doubted there was any more to know about Jesus. Instead of waiting for Jesus to appear in Jerusalem to His followers, they were going in the wrong direction.

This sounds like us. We hear reports of the Lord moving in power and grace in some other place, and it seems like nonsense to us. We want to believe. We want to trust Jesus for more, but it seems as though it will never happen for us. We've reached the limit of how deep we can go with Jesus. We believe that what we believe is all there is to believe. But the Master of our hearts knows full well where we're headed and where we need to go. Wanting them to go further with Him rather than backward, Jesus appeared to them on the Road to Emmaus.

Starting with Moses and the Prophets, Jesus opened their eyes to the truth, causing their hearts to burn within them. Although they were walking in the wrong direction, something in them changed as Jesus walked with them. Something will change in us as we go further with the Master. No matter how much we think we know about Him or how much we have experienced, there is more. Go further with Jesus. The apostle Paul reminds us: "Not that I have already obtained all this, or have already arrived at my goal, but I press on to take hold of that for which Christ Jesus took hold of me" (Philippians 3:12 NIV). When we think that we have come to the end of our knowing the fullness of Jesus, if we are willing to listen, we can hear the Lord speaking to us, "How foolish you are and how slow to believe."

As they approached the village to which they were going, Jesus continued on as if he were going farther. But they urged him strongly, "Stay with us, for it is nearly evening; the day is almost over." So he went in to stay with them (Luke 24:28–29, NIV).

> *Jesus first wanted to challenge their hearts, leading them to a place where they longed for more of His presence.*

What an incredible verse. The two followers of Jesus had completed their journey home, but Jesus appeared to be going farther. What would the men do? Would they let Him go? Would they go back to their old lives? Would they miss out on all that Jesus was willing to give?

Notice that only one of the followers is named. Cleopas was no doubt known by the Early Church. Some traditions say he was the brother of Joseph, Mary's husband. If that's true, Cleopas had no doubt seen Jesus many times before. But this time was different. They were kept from recognizing Jesus. Why would the Lord prevent them from knowing Him on the road? Why not simply appear to them, tell the great story of the Resurrection, and encourage them to spread the news? Perhaps Jesus first wanted to challenge their hearts, leading them to a place where they longed for more of His presence.

Countless times in my life, I've felt like one of the two on the road to Emmaus—confused and wondering why God hadn't worked things out the way I thought He should have. Yet each time, Jesus has asked me, "Will you go further with Me even when you don't understand?" Will I say yes to Jesus and reject the enemy's traps of doubt and fear?

As soon as Jesus revealed himself, they immediately ran back to Jerusalem and shared their amazing encounter with the other disciples who were still fearful and discouraged. Perhaps Jesus chose to appear to these two because they are us. He is calling us with the same passion and the same strong voice of love we heard when He first called us to follow Him. "Don't stop now," He is saying. "There is more. Go further."

ANSWER THE CALL

- What has happened in your life recently that has caused you to doubt, fear, mourn, or question God's plan for your life?

_____

_____

_____

_____

_____

- What can you do to put yourself in a position to hear from God again and experience His presence?

_____

_____

_____

_____

_____

GO FURTHER!

Ask God to reveal himself to you on whatever road you may be traveling. Ask Him to make your heart burn within you and make you long to go further with Him.

PRAY

Never Reached People Group: SINGAPORE'S SINHALESE

Pray that God will raise up and empower Sinhalese believers to build a strong church to reach their own people.

GO ANYWAY

John 21:15-19 ----------------------------

*When they had finished breakfast, Jesus said to Simon Peter, "Simon, son of John, do you love me more than these?" He said to him, "Yes, Lord; you know that I love you." He said to him, "Feed my lambs." He said to him a second time, "Simon, son of John, do you love me?" He said to him, "Yes, Lord; you know that I love you." He said to him, "Tend my sheep." He said to him the third time, "Simon, son of John, do you love me?" Peter was grieved because he said to him the third time, "Do you love me?" and he said to him, "Lord, you know everything; you know that I love you." Jesus said to him, "Feed my sheep. Truly, truly, I say to you, when you were young, you used to dress yourself and walk wherever you wanted, but when you are old, you will stretch out your hands, and another will dress you and carry you **where you do not want to go.**" (This he said to show by what kind of death he was to glorify God.) And after saying this he said to him, "Follow me." (ESV)*

Leaving Family Anyway

By Missy Towers, Indonesia

The pain of leaving behind these people and relationships makes me not want to go at all.

"Truly, truly, I say to you, when you were young, you used to dress yourself and walk wherever you wanted, but when you are old, you will stretch out your hands, and another will dress you and carry you where you do not want to go" (John 21:18, ESV).

Taking up our cross should encompass all of our being.

How would you feel if your teacher, who was just miraculously raised from the dead after a gruesome crucifixion, told you that you were going to die in the same manner? In the preceding verse, John explained that crucifixion was exactly what Jesus meant when He spoke to Peter. The Greek word used here for "to go" is *phero*. It's the same word used in Mark 15:22 to describe Jesus' going to Calvary. It's a word associated directly with crucifixion. The disciples would have known exactly what Jesus meant for Peter.

Jesus asks much of us. "If anyone would come after me, let him deny himself and take up his cross and follow me" (Mark 8:34). The consequences of following Jesus were clear: Peter would follow Christ to the cross.

Taking up our cross is not just a physical action. It should encompass all of our being—everything we are, everything we know, and everything we hold dear. Completing the Great Commission requires workers to go to dangerous, closed nations. Some will be martyred pursuing this goal. They will make the ultimate sacrifice so that others can hear. Each one of us should reflect on the possibility of martyrdom being at the end of our earthly path. Counting our costs is more than just a consideration of the silly, material things that clutter our homes or even meaningful relationships, although these are sacrifices we must make. Counting the cost requires grappling with paying with our lives so that others can hear God's truth.

One does not become a missionary to become wealthy. The job I left behind for my first missions assignment was not that great. I was educated as a journalist; giving up the pennies per word I would have earned writing stories for the local paper was not a great sacrifice. On the other hand, my husband is an engineer. The starting salary for a chemical engineer is more than most ever hope to make. A missionary's paycheck doesn't compare. Money and the things it buys don't really matter to me. Yes, I like cute shoes, but multiple pairs fit nicely in a suitcase.

The sacrifice that challenges me most is that of relationships. When my husband and I first felt the Lord stirring our hearts for global missions, we said, "We're young. We don't have any children. Let's go on this adventure with God." Two years later, the cute shoes in my suitcase have given way to the many items my baby boy will need while we're on the field.

My personal will, connected directly to God's intentions for my life, pushes me to reach the lost. My mom heart pushes back, telling me that taking my child so far from his grandparents is a horrible idea. My desire, placed in submission to God's, says to follow Him anywhere. As a daughter, it'll be difficult to give up my shopping trips with Mom.

Missionaries don't want to give these things up to go, but they go anyway. It's easier when we remember that our most important relationship is with Jesus. We don't want to hurt family and friends, but we certainly don't want to disappoint Jesus. Therefore, we go soberly, knowing the full weight of our decision.

I don't willingly take my son to a place where I'll have to travel to a *different* foreign country for medical care. I don't willingly place him in a situation where his relationships with extended family will be via a screen. I reluctantly leave my parents and our wonderful times together. Quite frankly, the pain of leaving behind these people and relationships makes me not want to go at all.

I don't believe Christ willingly went to the cross. Yes, He knew the Father's will. He knew what had to be done. But the difficulty of the sacrifice required brought reluctance. Jesus pleaded, "Father, if you are willing, please take this cup of suffering from me. Yet I want your will to be done, not mine" (Luke 22:42, NLT).

Redeeming mankind required Jesus' death. He knew the agonizing torture He would endure, yet He still went to the cross for me. Knowing that, should I be any less willing? I am, but I go anyway.

Jesus warned Peter what was coming. He also promised Peter would play a key part in building the church: "You are Peter (which means 'rock'), and upon this rock I will build my church, and all the powers of hell will not conquer it" (Matthew 16:18).

Reluctance is OK as long as we go anyway. It means we've counted the costs, the sacrifices we must make. My human heart tells me not to go there. But because of what God has done, I go anyway.

ANSWER THE CALL

- What would be hardest for you to sacrifice to follow God without reservation?

_____

_____

_____

_____

_____

- Missionary Jim Elliot wrote, "He is no fool who gives what he cannot keep to gain that which he cannot lose." How does it help to remember that those things we most try to protect are not ours to keep?

_____

_____

_____

_____

_____

GO ANYWAY!

Listen to (or read the lyrics) of Keith Green's song, "Pledge My Head to Heaven." Come to terms with the sacrifices any believer might be called upon to make for the gospel through prayer. Then write your own pledge.

PRAY

Never Reached People Group: INDONESIA'S KEPULAUAN SULA

Ask God to send more workers so that no Kepulauan Sula man, woman, or child will remain never reached by the gospel.

Where You Do Not Want to Go

By Rebekah Zeiler, Cambodia

Nay-uhk-jit-khan roe-boh khey-nom means "the neighbor that belongs to me."

We live in a concrete townhouse in Phnom Penh. The walls rattle when ceaseless planes fly overhead. There's constant construction. Everything is made of concrete, metal and tile, and we feel every rotation of the tile saw, every tat-tat-tat of the hammer drill.

My neighbors on the left place offerings to the spirits at the foot of the trees on our plot. They have two altars in their house and one on their porch. I would like to say that I'm not afraid, but I am. "When I am afraid, I will put my trust in you" (Psalm 56:3, NLT).

For some reason, these neighbors don't like us. They barely respond to our greetings. This is difficult for me because I'm your dessert-sharing, help-you-with-whatever kind of neighbor.

My neighbor had a baby—a beautiful baby boy with round cheeks and light, chocolatey-brown skin—named Nano. We told them he is handsome, because he is. Maybe my youngest child will befriend him, and something will be better. Perhaps, one day, my Khmer will be good enough to say, "Let's be friends," and have them over for dinner.

Meanwhile, I just want to move. It's so loud I'm crying. I want a house without tile saws, banging, shaking, hammer drills and airplanes. I'm daydreaming about my imaginary house again in the English countryside or the foothills of Switzerland—with a babbling brook and a forest with all the lush green trees, and open fields of all the wildest of wildflowers one could imagine... with wooden floors and arched ceilings like a cathedral, and exposed wooden beams... and a glass window seat for reading overlooking a garden....a big open kitchen, with a fireplace in it ...a deep soaking bathtub, and a terrace to have coffee and devotional time with Jesus in the mornings, while there is still dew on the ground, and the sun is just starting to break through...

The sewer pipes break again. We can't flush the toilet until it's fixed. Water from the kitchen sink is pouring onto the floor. All the bleach in Belgium won't make the mold smell go away.

We tell our mentors. They understand our housing problems are real. They're kind and supportive because sewage in the living room is not OK. They validate us because it is so, so loud. They tell us to do whatever we need to do to make it here. They also remind us: "When you moved in, you told us you felt this was where God wanted you to be." We remember too. It doesn't sit well with me.

It's Friday around lunchtime. Our neighbor, the daddy, paces slowly on the back porch, rocking the baby. I think, *He's a good daddy. He loves his baby.*

Day turns to night. Brett steps outside to take a call, then returns. "I think our neighbor's baby died."

I'm terrified. Tears flow. My mind runs in a million directions— we have to move; we can't stay here; we have to go outside.

When we go outside, we see straw mats with bowls of fruit, cans of beer, bao buns stuck with smoldering incense sticks, and burning candles. Cambodians gather in the dark on the driveway in that distinct, hushed sadness that hovers when there is a death.

Brett has learned the Khmer expression of condolence. I repeat it to myself again and again as we slip off our shoes and enter their house, but I can't hold it in my head. On the living room floor, the deceased baby lies by a wooden burial box. His older siblings crouch stoically nearby with tear-filled, reddened eyes.

The neighbor that belongs to me comes toward me, clutches me close, and sobs. I sob and embrace her. I whisper, "Jesus," again and again. A dozen Cambodians stare at me. Why would this foreigner care?

Then, to my unconcealed surprise, the neighbor that belongs to me starts speaking—in English. "The baby had a heart problem," she says. "Too small."

I tell her we are Christians. I tell her we will pray.

I cry myself to sleep.

That weekend, at a missions conference in Thailand, they tell us about culture fatigue—where you want to give up because so many horrible things are crashing in on each other. And now the guest speaker is preaching about...houses!?

From one man he made every nation of men, that they should inhabit the whole earth; and he determined the times set for them and the exact places where they should live (Acts 17:26, NIV).

Why is he talking about houses? God ordained the exact places people live? Can't we just talk about having joy or something? On the corner of my notes, I write to Brett, "We aren't supposed to move." He sighs; he knows it too.

Back home, the construction continues. We take our neighbor flowers because when your baby dies, someone should give you flowers. But truly, what do you give someone when their precious baby dies?

That evening, the woman who lost her baby but a few days ago is standing on my back step holding out food to me. More hugs. I cry over Khmer curry. It's delicious.

----

*It's not where we
wanted to go. But Jesus
asks us to go here,
so we go anyway.*

The next day, the walls are banging and reverberating. My neighbor sends me a picture of her baby's grave with bottles of milk on it. And dead chickens. And offerings for the spirits.

Later, she sends me a message that she is crying. I ask if she wants to talk. She says yes, so we sit and talk about Nano. She shows me a beautiful picture of sweet Nano, which she says means "the smallest one." On the porch of our conjoined houses, we just sit. She offers to take me to the open-air market with her. She too hates the airplanes that fly overhead constantly.

I use all my Khmer words, but her English is really good. We talk about Jesus. She listens and asks questions. She is mourning. No mama should lose a baby.

I ask if I can pray, and she says yes.

Holding her hands, I pray. She fights back tears. She talks about suffering, and I tell her about Jesus, who suffered and died for us. We talk for a long time.

"Do you like living here?" she asks me.

I pause. I tell her—or maybe I tell myself—"I like being your neighbor. I think I'm supposed to tell you about Preah Jesu." She nods. I tell her I love her. She says she loves me, too. She hasn't accepted Jesus—yet. But she's listening. I'm listening too. Maybe that's the point of noise: to silence the whispers of the Holy Spirit, the only One who can bring peace into this dark place.

I don't understand tragedy, but I do know this: Jesus loves the neighbor that belongs to me. He loves precious baby Nano. And we love our neighbors. We are where we belong. It's not where we wanted to go. But Jesus asks us to go here, so we go anyway.

ANSWER THE CALL

- Are you where you belong?

_____

_____

_____

_____

_____

- Avoid the distraction of longing for a better place. Choose to focus on who you can minister to where Christ has placed you today.

_____

_____

_____

_____

_____

GO ANYWAY!

Find a way to silence the noise of life and seek God's face. Look for evidence of His calling and working through you in the place you have been reluctant to go or remain. Ask God to give you grace as you go anyway.

PRAY

Never Reached People Group: CAMBODIA'S WESTERN CHAM

Ask God to prepare the hearts of the Cham for the coming of the gospel and the hearts of workers to go and tell them.

The Price

What is Jesus asking you to surrender so others can find freedom?

Why is my lot so hard and theirs so easy?

"Why?" threatens to drown out "Go!"

We were shocked when cancer came knocking on our door as a young family in our first missions term. My husband had been sick for months while doctors tried to determine the cause. A CT Scan revealed a dense mass in his intestine that was almost certainly cancer. The moment I heard the word cancer, time stood still. I couldn't catch my breath.

When frontline realities shatter romanticized missionary dreams, what does the Lord require? Missionary life is a delicate balance of pursuing God's call and clinging to hope while battling evil. The enemy knows God is sending ambassadors to people in darkness. When you become God's diplomat, the enemy turns his attention to you. Never reached people are enslaved by Satan, and he won't release them without a fight.

Saying yes to Jesus requires denying ourselves, taking up our cross, and following Jesus in self-sacrifice (Matthew 16:24). Our commitment to Christ clearly entails death. Before arriving on the field, one thinks blessings await the brave missionary. Then suffering comes. You desperately pray over your delirious child or are shocked by your 34-year-old husband's cancer diagnosis. "Why?" threatens to drown out "Go!" Maybe you shouldn't have uprooted your family and moved halfway around the globe. The enemy whispers: "You gave it a good try. No one will blame you for going home. You aren't cut out for this."

Simon Peter's induction into Kingdom service came with full disclosure that it would end in death. Jesus had chosen Peter as the rock on which He would build the church (Matthew 16:18), but that privilege came with a price. When Jesus reaffirmed Peter's call, He outlined the cost:

"When you were younger you dressed yourself and went where you wanted; but when you are old you will stretch out your hands, and someone else will dress you and lead you where you do not want to go" (John 21:18, NIV).

Peter's response to this death sentence was not to negotiate or pledge his loyalty to Jesus. Instead, Peter pointed to John and asked, "What about him?" How many times have I asked Jesus this exact question? What about him? How about her? I've given You everything. Why is my lot so hard and theirs so easy?" In those moments of self-pity and grief, Jesus lovingly answers me just as He did Peter, "What is that to you? You must follow Me."

What is Jesus asking you to surrender so others can find freedom? When the nations cry out for deliverance, the Lord of the harvest sends laborers. He chooses those willing to go when the going gets rough. There is a price for reconciling the lost to the Father. God's ambassadors must sacrifice the safe haven of our homeland and walk roads of heartach and sorrow. We must ask the Holy Spirit to fortify us with supernatural strength and endurance.

When he returned from the hospital, I had a vision of a hand resting below my heart, suppressing my fears, worries and anxieties. After the doctor discovered the mass, God asked us to trust His knowledge as He ordered our steps. We did not expect such grace or strength from the Father as we experienced during that time.

An unmistakable peace rested over us as we walked into the doctor's office to hear the results. Turning her computer screen to us, the doctor showed a noticeable black mass on the CT scan, and then walked us through all 15 pictures from the colonoscopy. To her surprise, the mass was *gone*!

Later my dear friend, who waited with me during the procedure, told me the most miraculous part of the whole ordeal wasn't the amazing miracle of healing, but witnessing the supernatural peace I had that day.

I'm convinced that signs and wonders are secondary to walking through hardships with the tangible peace of Christ. The vast majority of people in our area of the world have never met a Christian. They draw opinions about Christianity from government actions or Hollywood movies. There simply aren't opportunities to observe the indescribable peace of Christ within their cultural context. The never reached people of the world will only be reached when we draw a line in the sand and declare, "We do not belong to those who shrink back and are destroyed, but to those who have faith and are saved" (Hebrews 10:39). At times, God's straight and narrow path for our lives look broken and dangerous. Refuse to shrink back. Jesus said, "I have told you these things, so that in me you may have peace. In this world you will have trouble. But take heart I have overcome the world" (John 16:33).

Nations are waiting on the other side of your obedience. Choose to go. Jesus will never leave or forsake you. He will restore your joy and confidence to reap a plentiful harvest. The ends of the earth await salvation. Follow God's call, even through the valleys. Don't permit the enemy to disqualify you. It takes guts to push through to see the promises of God brought to completion. Allow the breath of God to restore your dry and weary bones. Don't give up! Go anyway, and you will see God's glory unfold.

ANSWER THE CALL

- What price have you paid to share the gospel?

_____

_____

_____

_____

_____

- What price are you willing to pay?

_____

_____

_____

_____

_____

GO ANYWAY!

Write a note, make a phone call, or pay a visit to encourage a missionary or other worker who may be going through a difficult time. Ask God for a special Bible verse, word, or gesture of kindness you can share with them. Thank them for their service and commit to praying for them.

PRAY

Never Reached People Group: ETHNIC CHINESE THAI

Ask God to arrange for Chinese Thai individuals to have divine appointments with Christ followers, wherever they may go.

Washing Our Father's Dishes

By Dick Brogden, Live Dead Arab World

Energy spent wondering what others are doing or not doing is wasted.

As followers of Jesus, we have been invited into His mission.

Pentecostal missiology has always been linked to eschatology. We've understood that our only hope is when Jesus comes, and we've felt the urgency of Matthew 24:14: "This gospel of the kingdom will be preached in all the world as a witness to all the nations, and then the end will come" (NKJV). Knowing we are weak, longing for Jesus to come, our faith fathers and mothers fell on their knees and pleaded for the power of the Holy Spirit. Why? So they could preach the gospel among every people as a witness. And why do that? So the end will come, and we can all be with Jesus—for, as Paul said, that indeed is far better (Philippians 1:23).

When I was a child, I loved Christmas—I still do. In the weeks before Christmas, my parents would wrap the presents and put them under the tree. The family tradition was to open our presents early on Christmas morning, and my sisters and I would rise eager to open them.

If my father had said to me early on Christmas morning, "These dishes of the kitchen will be washed, and all the table cleaned as a witness, and then the end of all waiting will come, and then we will open our presents," I would have sprinted to the kitchen as fast as I could. I would have mobilized my sisters and flung myself into action. I don't like doing dishes, but I love getting Christmas presents!

As followers of Jesus, we have been invited into His mission. This is true for all believers, not only for missionaries who serve far from home. What happens to my brother or sister is not my main concern; my main focus is eternal life with Jesus. I must fling myself into the actions the Father has required for Jesus to come. The grandest present of them all, unbroken and eternal intimate union with Jesus himself—no sin and no curse—is waiting for us. All we have to do is run to the kitchen and wash the Father's dishes. All we have to do is preach the gospel of the Kingdom among every nation as a witness—and then the King will come.

John 21:21–25 contains the closing verses of the Gospel, and while they don't contain an explicit commission to the nations (as does every other Gospel in their closing verses (Matthew 28:19–20; Mark 16:15–18; Luke 24:46–49), there is the implicit commission in John 20:21 ("As the Father has sent me, I also send you") and the personal commission to Peter in John 21:15–19 ("Feed my lambs, tend my sheep, feed my sheep, llow me"). On the heels of being given personal instructions and a hint f personal cost, Peter inquired what would happen to John, as if to ask, "What price will John pay? Do I alone have to bear the burden? Do I alone ave to pay the price?" Jesus answers bluntly:

"If I will that he remain till I come, what is that to you? You follow Me" *John 21:22).*

Such questions are not Peter's concern. Quibbling about who does hat, who pays what price, and what is fair is not how we should spend ur energy—the divine will determines those answers. We are to have but ne focus—following Jesus, being sent as He was sent, and laying down ur lives that the gospel might go to the uttermost parts of the earth. ather than comparing ourselves, our work, and our fate to others, we are ɔ concentrate on our simple assignment.

We must constantly resist the distraction of questioning what other eople are doing. We've been given a great responsibility to the never ached, and we must be faithful. We begin in a focused fashion, but efore long, we begin to tire at the enormity of the task and shift our focus rom the field to our friends. "Why is that one not working as hard as I am? Vhy is this one doing such stupid stuff?" We can easily become resentful, ritical, judgmental, competitive, jealous and cranky. We feel ignored. We an become ambitious for power. We can start to act competitively. We can lide into comparison, insecurity and self-pity. And to us who, in myriad ifferent ways, ask Jesus about others or mutter about them under our ɾeath, Jesus bluntly says: "What is that to you? You follow Me."

Jesus tells us to mind our own business and reminds us of the end ɟoal—His coming. Our attention should never be on others, but on Him, His mission, and our assignment to wash the Father's dishes—to preach he gospel to every people group. Only then will the end come. Energy pent wondering about what others are doing or not doing is wasted ɛnergy. Let's hasten the day of His coming by hastening away from vondering about others' faults and fate.

Let's not forget the beauty and the privilege of our call as believers. ɛt not the follies, failures or fantastic accomplishments of others in life listract us from our assignment. Let's commit once again to focusing our ɛnergy on making disciples where there are none and planting churches vhere they don't exist. With urgency and joy for the reward set before us, et's take our eyes off our colleagues and critics and fix them on the fields, he lost, and the coming King.

ANSWER THE CALL

- Some are called to go, others to send. What is Jesus calling you to do?

  _____

  _____

  _____

  _____

- What feeling, annoyance or unfairness has been distracting you from single-minded focus on the task of fulfilling the Great Commission?

  _____

  _____

  _____

  _____

- What can you do to keep your focus off others and on Christ and the work He has called you to do?

  _____

  _____

  _____

  _____

GO ANYWAY!

If you are struggling with feelings of unfairness, lack of recognition and praise, or frustration, write down or articulate your honest concerns and questions. Imagine Jesus' response: "What is that to you? You follow Me." Ask God to renew your focus on Him and on what is truly important.

PRAY

Never Reached People Group: THE BAKUMPAI OF INDONESIA

Ask God for a spiritual breakthrough among the Bakumpai that would dispel centuries of spiritual darkness with the light of the gospel.

Reluctant Heroes

By Cari Hurst

Choosing to follow Jesus wholeheartedly is a deliberate act of subjugating our own will to his.

Captain Ferrier didn't want to pilot the doomed plane into the ground, but he did it anyway.

Captain John Ferrier didn't want to die that day. The respected combat pilot had a wife and three children. When his F-86 Sabrejet malfunctioned while executing the "bomb burst" maneuver with the Air National Guard's Jet Precision Demonstration Team, he could have saved himself by ejecting. But, if he had, the pilotless jet would have crashed into a small town nearby, killing and injuring many on the ground. Bravely, he chose to save the lives of others rather than his own. Captain Ferrier didn't want to pilot the doomed plane into the ground, but he did it anyway.

People like Captain Ferrier, who made the choice to save others even at the cost of his own life, are heroes. Such people show real courage—and love. As Jesus said, "Greater love has no one than this: to lay down one's life for one's friends" (John 15:13, NIV). Like this brave pilot, missionaries might not personally know the people for whom they are called to sacrifice, but they still lay down their lives for a friend—Jesus.

Facing the prospect of our own death is difficult, even for followers of Jesus Christ, who will spend eternity with Him. Even when we understand the purpose of the sacrifice we are called to make...even when we make it on behalf of our friend, Jesus, who gave His life for us, no matter how loving and brave we may be, our strong self-preservation instincts cause us to do all that we can to escape death. Jesus himself, who was fully divine as well as fully human, struggled in the face of His upcoming suffering and death on the cross: "Overcome with grief, he threw himself facedown on the ground and prayed, 'My Father, if there is any way you can deliver me from this suffering, please take it from me'" (Matthew 26:39, The Passion Translation).

I'm grateful the verse didn't end with Jesus' struggle. In spite of His human aversion to pain and suffering, Jesus embraced the Father's plan of redemption and expressed His commitment to playing His role no matter how difficult. "Yet what I want is not important, for I only desire to fulfill your plan for me" (Matthew 26:39). As followers of Jesus, we are called to no less.

After His resurrection, Jesus recommissioned Simon Peter for service. But He also gave Peter a glimpse of the way he would ultimately die—following his Lord in crucifixion.

"'When you were younger, you used to gird yourself and walk wherever you wished; but when you grow old, you will stretch out your hands and someone else will gird you, and bring you where you do not wish to go.' Now this He said, signifying by what kind of death he would glorify God. And when He had spoken this, He said to Him, 'Follow me!'" (John 21:18–19, NASB).

In that moment, Peter had a choice—would he follow Jesus no matter the cost, even knowing that it would mean a painful death in the end? At Jesus' urging, Peter said yes. He chose to follow Jesus anyway. This brings me hope because Peter had a track record of hesitation and faltering (remember walking on the water in the storm and his denials of Christ?). There have been many times in my own life where I've heard the call to go, and my initial response was doubt, fear and hesitation. I'm so thankful I chose to go anyway. Often our biggest struggles are not against circumstances or problems facing us but are within us. God gives us a choice and free will. Choosing to follow Jesus wholeheartedly is a deliberate act of subjugating our own will to His.

Almost 16 years ago, I stood before family and friends and publicly declared *I will* to the man who was to be my husband. Ever since, I've had to choose daily whether to be faithful, supportive, loving and kind. We have the same choice in our daily walk with Jesus. Missionaries don't go to foreign lands to tell others about Jesus because they want to sacrifice, suffer and die. But they go anyway. They honor their commitment to following their friend, Jesus, by being willing to lay down their lives for Him. They resolve to finish the mission, no matter the cost.

Here are some lessons I've learned along the way:

- God has called us all to follow Him, but each of our paths is different.

- Completing our mission may lead to death, but that death brings glory to God (John 21:19).

- Following Christ requires dying to self and living selflessly.

- Going in obedience to Christ's call doesn't guarantee a life of ease, but it does guarantee a life of fulfillment.

- It's OK to go reluctantly, but you must go anyway. Otherwise, you're not really following Jesus.

NSWER THE CALL

- What does Jesus' call, "Follow me," mean to you personally?

_____

_____

_____

_____

_____

- What makes you most reluctant to answer the Christ's call?

_____

_____

_____

_____

_____

GO ANYWAY!

It's human nature to want to avoid suffering, pain and death. That's why we must daily die to our old human nature and put on the nature of Christ. Read 2 Corinthians 5, and consider how it relates to the believer's call to follow Christ wherever He may lead, even to places of great suffering and death.

PRAY

Never Reached People Group: THE SAMA-BAJAU (PHILIPPINES)
Pray for a mighty move of the Spirit among the Sama-Bajau people that will open the hearts of many to Christ in your lifetime.

GO WAIT

Acts 1:1-5 ---

In the first book, O Theophilus, I have dealt with all that Jesus began to do and teach, until the day when he was taken up, after he had given commands through the Holy Spirit to the apostles whom he had chosen. He presented himself alive to them after his suffering by many proofs, appearing to them during forty days and speaking about the kingdom of God.

*And while staying with them he ordered them not to depart from Jerusalem, but to **wait for the promise of the Father**, which, he said, "you heard from me; for John baptized with water, but you will be baptized with the Holy Spirit not many days from now." (ESV)*

The Act of Waiting

By Jonathan Lowrance, Japan

Life's best blessings often are born not from the easiest but the most challenging tasks.

"Wait for the gift my Father promised" (Acts 1:4, NIV).

Waiting isn't idleness; it's a passionate pursuit of God.

As a child, I hated waiting for anything. Waiting requires patience, and I had little of that. "When I'm an adult, things will be different," I told myself. Little did I know that the most difficult times of waiting would come as an adult. Waiting has always been difficult, yet Jesus spent a great deal of His time on earth waiting. He spent 30 years waiting—a wait that culminated in a challenging 40-day fast and temptation in the wilderness. That period of intense waiting launched Him into full-time ministry. Frankly, waiting is hard. However, life's best blessings often are born not from the easiest but the most challenging tasks. Perhaps you're experiencing one of those trying times in your life right now. I pray that as we focus on two distinct aspects of waiting, you'll once again feel the stirring of hope.

Waiting is not passive—it's not a holding pattern of sorts. Waiting requires the kind of action that strategically positions us to receive wisdom, direction and empowerment from God. Before ascending to heaven, Jesus told His followers to wait for the gift promised by God. But that didn't mean they should do nothing. While waiting in the Upper Room together, they prayed and sought God. This action—drawing near to God—positioned them spiritually to receive the gift of the Holy Spirit. Waiting isn't idleness; it's a passionate pursuit of God.

Our impression of God during seasons of waiting is critical; it will either drive our pursuit or cause us to lose heart at a crucial moment. When it feels like our life has been put on pause, God isn't withholding answers. Paul reminds us, "In all things God works for the good of those who love him, who have been called according to his purpose" (Romans 8:28). Our feelings can be a poor litmus test for God's activity. Instead, stand on the promises of His Word. He has not forsaken you or forgotten about your future. Even as you sleep at night, He is working for your good.

Waiting has a purpose. My wife and I had been serving as young adult leaders at a church for seven years. We knew we were called to full-time ministry, but out of necessity, we worked secular jobs as we prayed for God to give us direction. Long years of waiting with no clear direction brought frustration. Fear began to consume me, quenching any spark of hope.

felt purposeless and unfulfilled. Over time, my worship grew empty and forced, yet, I continued to offer it up to God in hopes that the fire, which seemed to be dying inside, would once again be rekindled. Had I missed something? Had God changed His mind?

During this time, my wife and I decided to take a dream vacation in Japan. We were fascinated by the culture. We began scrimping and saving every penny for the expensive trip. We were serving as missions directors at our church when missionaries from Japan brought us some material. I wept uncontrollably when their DVD told that less than 1 percent of the Japanese population knows Christ as Savior. I'd never felt anything like that emotion. After years of waiting, God finally began to speak to me. The fog of uncertainty began to lift, and in its place, clarity was restored. The trip to Japan, the missionary's DVD, and the indescribable burden for the Japanese people that had hit me like a lightning bolt from heaven convinced me of one inescapable truth: God was calling us to be missionaries to Japan. The puzzle pieces that had remained so elusive suddenly clicked into place. Patiently and lovingly, God helped us take the necessary steps to get to this point.

This experience taught me two lessons. First, sometimes, in spite of how we might feel, we're not ready for God's next step. I realized that God's plan for my life was so big that, had He revealed it sooner, I wouldn't have accepted it. You see, long ago, when I first committed my life to work for Him, I prayed, "God, I'll do whatever You want me to do. But if You want me to be a missionary, please change my heart." Changes needed to take place within me, and God was answering my prayers. He brought my desires into alignment with His through a period of waiting. What God did in my heart during that period went beyond bringing me to a place of acceptance—it instilled in me a burning desire and excitement for reaching the Japanese people. I couldn't get on a plane fast enough.

The second lesson was that every part of God's plan has a specifically designed purpose, including the wait. As I look back on what felt like a tortuous time in my life, I now see it with a heart of humility and thankfulness. As we wait, God may be working in our circumstances as well as our hearts. He may be working in people, places and financial matters in ways necessary for our success in the new season we are about to enter. When we're waiting, it's easy to forget that God's timing is perfect. But know that, whatever you're praying for, God has already determined the exact time and place for the answer to come. Don't lose heart. Keep praying, keep believing, and trust Him with the timing.

ANSWER THE CALL

- What are you waiting for from God?

  _____

  _____

  _____

  _____

  _____

- What evidence have you seen of His working in your life?

  _____

  _____

  _____

  _____

  _____

GO WAIT!

Talk to and pray with a friend or spiritual mentor about your frustrations with waiting. Sometimes it helps to see our situation from another person's perspective, as they may help us connect some dots we may be overlooking.

PRAY

Never Reached People Group: OKINAWAN RYUKYUAN

Pray for believers at work among the Okinawan Ryukyuan, that they and their families may have wisdom, courage, stamina, provision, favor, protection and grace as ambassadors of Christ's love.

Longevity

Sometimes we just have to dig in our heels and determine to wait.

After five years of waiting and building relationships with Buddhist and animist friends around us, something suddenly shifted in the spirit realm.

We live in a world where we can have almost anything we want delivered to our front door, often in a matter of minutes. Hungry? Two clicks on an app, and dinner and groceries come to your door. Don't like what's on TV? No problem! Stream anything you want at the click of a button. We rarely have to wait for anything. Because of this, waiting can be one of the most difficult things to do. Yet, in His last words to His disciples, Jesus told them to wait.

"Wait for the gift my Father promised, which you have heard me speak about...In a few days you will be baptized with the Holy Spirit" *(Acts 1:4–5, NIV).*

After Jesus went to heaven, His followers could have immediately tried to preach and teach the things they'd heard and seen Him do. But Jesus told them to wait for power from the Holy Spirit to be His witnesses. They chose to obey and wait for Jesus' promised gift. Because they waited, thousands believed and were baptized in a very short time.

When we first arrived in this closed Asian country, we had little more than a promise that God would use us to share His message with the never reached in these remote mountains. We didn't have a detailed outline of how it would all come together, but we believed a promise that we would lead Bible studies, train disciples, and see lives changed through the power of the Holy Spirit.

Because of government restrictions, we were not allowed to openly share with the lost people we encountered every day. We were not able to have small groups or meetings with those who had never heard the name of Christ. Every time we tried to start a Bible study with even the few believers that we had met, something stopped it from happening. In the midst of that discouraging time, the Holy Spirit reassured us that He was working all around us and that His timing was perfect. We just needed to wait.

After five years of waiting and building relationships with Buddhist and animist friends around us, something suddenly shifted in the spirit realm. More and more, we were able to share one on one with our friends. All of a sudden, we were ready to launch our first Bible study with unbelievers. The promise of the Father had come!

For almost six months, we led a Bible study with our indigenous friend. They listened as we walked through the Bible explaining God as Creator, Savior, and Healer. No one said much, and I began to question why they kept coming when they hardly seemed interested in our discussions. I even wondered if we had missed God in starting the Bible study. Finally, our animist friend, Loy, shared his story. I sat in awe as he began to tell of all the Father had been doing in his heart during the last six months.

Loy had grown up in the mountains. He was exposed to Christianity by his parents, who were believers, although he never had the chance to decide to follow Christ himself. He had been waiting for 30 years, since his parents' death, for someone to come and tell him how he could follow Jesus as his parents had. With a beautiful smile on his face, he told us that he was now following Christ. Now he knew he would see his parents again, in heaven.

I had been looking at Loy's face for evidence of God's work in his life, when we all know God's work always begins in the unseen realms of the heart. God had been working in Loy's life long before I met him. Every conversation was leading Loy to the feet of Jesus. What little faith I'd had to lose hope in the promise of the Father.

Sometimes we just have to dig in our heels and determine to wait. About three years after we arrived, God planted the idea of longevity deep in my heart. Working among those who know so little of Jesus is difficult and exhausting. The enemy wants us to feel like it's hopeless. We must be committed to persevere in hard places. We must keep tilling soil that's hard and dry. We must dig in our heels and be determined to keep tilling, planting and watering the seeds of the gospel.

Loy is still discovering who Jesus is for himself. His hunger to learn more about the Father is beautiful, and he has true joy. Because we waited for the right time to start the weekly Bible study, the seeds that were planted in Loy's heart when he was a young boy have brought forth an eternal harvest. He has experienced salvation and even been miraculously healed of a growth on his ear. Today, Loy constantly shares the message of Jesus, his Savior and Healer.

No matter what you are waiting on God for, know that His timing is always perfect. Because of Loy's decision to follow Christ and his position in the government, we now have freedom to lead small group Bible studies with students, even in this closed communist nation. This never could have happened before.

Let's join with the disciples and be determined to wait on the promise of the Father. If we will believe and not give up hope, we will see a harvest.

ANSWER THE CALL

- Have you chosen to wait for the power of the Holy Spirit in your life?

_____

_____

_____

_____

- What personal example have you seen of God's working long before you were aware of it?

_____

_____

_____

_____

- Why do we still lose hope when we have seen God's faithfulness in the past?

_____

_____

_____

_____

GO WAIT!

Recount instances of God's past faithfulness to you or to others. Ask God to give you patience and faith as you wait for Him to move in your present circumstances. Take some time today to wait in God's presence asking Him to empower you through the Holy Spirit.

PRAY

Never Reached People Group: THE PHU THAI

Ask God to reveal himself to the Phu Thai people through dreams and visions.

Our Waiting Year

By Rachel Powell, Thailand

As we wait on the Lord, we receive power.

Jesus was alive! His followers were eager to tell everyone the news as the first missionaries. But what amazing Spirit-led instructions did Jesus give them? Wait.

"Wait for the gift my Father promised, which you have heard me speak about. For John baptized with water, but in a few days you will be baptized with the Holy Spirit" (Acts 1:4–5, NIV).

Like a muscle, patience is developed over time. While patience does develop as we grow, impatience is not reserved for young children. I'm still working daily to develop more patience. This can be very challenging, because patience seems to counteract purpose. However, the Bible shows us that there is purpose in patience. If we don't slow down, we can miss God's purpose for us.

Recently, I've learned a lot about the importance of waiting. In college, I felt the Holy Spirit calling me to be a missionary. It was exciting, and also a little scary. A few years later, my husband and I knew it was time. We prayed, prepared, and applied to be missionaries to Thailand. We also learned we were expecting our second child. Life was good.

Three days before our first missionary interview, I was admitted to the hospital with breathing problems, where I was told that I had stage III lung cancer. It was like a punch to the stomach that completely took our breath away. How could this happen? We tried to move forward with the missions process, but as we talked more with leaders, we knew it was time to wait.

In August, I had major surgery to remove a large tumor and my entire left lung, all while I was 10 weeks pregnant. It was the scariest time of our lives. We had such uncertainty—and there was so much waiting. We had no idea what the future would look like. Would I need chemotherapy or other treatment? How would my breathing be affected with only one lung?

After a few weeks in the hospital, I was released to go home. I was doing well, and the tiny life inside of me was doing great. We felt we could finally move on, focusing on getting healthy and getting to Thailand. Being a young, healthy person with no other medical issues, doctors believed I would recover quickly without any other treatment. This was such a relief to hear.

Yet weeks passed, then months, and I wasn't getting better. In fact, I was getting worse. I spent most of my days unable to get off the couch or out of bed. My sleeping patterns were a mess, and I had difficulty sleeping. I couldn't eat much of anything. I was losing weight, which was a major

When the disciples obeyed Jesus and waited the Holy Spirit came in power.

concern for my pregnancy. Soon I was having episodes of fever and chills, accompanied by a rapid heart rate.

In October, two months after this ordeal had begun, I was back in the hospital. Doctors were concerned with my bloodwork but were unsure what exactly was causing my health issues. After many painful tests, they discovered that had a serious infection from surgery. Had it entered my bloodstream, t would've been deadly for both me and my baby. Thankfully, doctors ound it in time and scheduled me for another surgery. Although I was hankful to have an answer, another surgery was a disappointing setback.

After two more surgeries and almost three weeks in the hospital, I was inally making progress. On the ride home from the hospital, I ate my first real meal in almost two months without getting sick. Praise God! After four more weeks on antibiotics, I was finally feeling healthier with each passing day. In February, we had a perfectly healthy baby girl.

One year after my last surgery, we were approved as missionaries to Thailand. As we prepared to go, we knew that this was the perfect time. Although my battle with cancer had seemed like an unwarranted delay, God perfectly orchestrated everything in His timing.

I like to think of that time as our waiting year. We knew God had called us to be missionaries, but it was as if He said to us, "Go, but wait." Much like the disciples in Acts, we knew the hope and power of the gospel and felt ready to share it. Yet, Jesus intended for us to wait. What happened when the disciples obeyed Jesus and waited? The Holy Spirit came in power.

Jesus promised in Acts 1:5 that if the disciples waited, they would be baptized in the Holy Spirit. Jesus promised, "You will receive power when the Holy Spirit comes upon you. And you will be my witnesses, telling people about me everywhere—in Jerusalem, throughout Judea, in Samaria, and to the ends of the earth" (Acts 1:8, NLT).

The Holy Spirit fell as they waited, baptizing them. The Bible says that "everyone present was filled with the Holy Spirit and began speaking in other languages" (Acts 2:4). In that moment, they began declaring the gospel in languages they didn't know. Because they had listened and obeyed Jesus by waiting, they received power from the Spirit, and the gospel spread farther than they ever thought possible.

Power comes in waiting. As we wait on the Lord, we receive power and learn what makes His heart beat. In obedient waiting, we become more like Him. Time waiting is not time wasted. Only after such waiting are we truly ready to go.

ANSWER THE CALL

- What have you learned from your times of waiting?

_____

_____

_____

_____

- Carve out some time today to wait on God. In a quiet moment listen for what God is speaking to your heart. Ask God to give you power to complete the work He wants you to do.

_____

_____

_____

_____

- Who do you know who might benefit from hearing your story of God's faithfulness during a time of waiting?

_____

_____

_____

_____

GO WAIT!

Develop your patience by delaying gratification. Put off that impulse buy. Skip that snack. Do one more chore before quitting. Ask God to give you urgency to go tell others about Him but patience to wait for His proper timing.

PRAY

Never Reached People Group: THAILAND'S MON

Pray for miracles, signs and wonders among Thailand's Mon people that will point them to our powerful God who loves them.

The Time In Between

Something happened in the waiting.

"Were you praying for me?" Of course I'd been praying—the man's ear was bleeding. I looked at him with tired eyes. I was weary from waiting. Waiting to board the plane, waiting for repairs to be made, waiting in line for new tickets after my flight got canceled, and waiting for this new flight.

A few hours before, I'd just gotten settled on a plane to Chicago. No one was seated beside me, and I'd decided to sleep during the flight. I hadn't slept much since getting the call that my grandmother had died.

Waiting is one of the hard things about life. But we aren't the first to experience the frustration of waiting. After Jesus rose from the dead, He instructed His disciples:

"Wait for the gift my Father promised" (Acts 1:4, NIV).

Jesus had died, He conquered death, and before leaving them for heaven, He told them to wait in Jerusalem for an unspecified amount of time for an unknown event to occur. These guys had laid down their aspirations, means of livelihood, families, and homes to follow Jesus. (That feels oddly familiar.) They left everything to answer the call, and their leader was brutally killed. Then, after His resurrection, when they were most enthused, Jesus told them to wait. (I relate to that, too). Imagine what it must have felt like to be commanded to wait when what you really wanted to do was go tell the world amazing news.

I imagine it felt something like going to missions orientation, committing to lay down your former life, getting pumped to take the gospel around the world, and then going home and spending the next year raising your budget. It might have felt like raising your budget to go to the country of your calling and spending the next year in language school. It might have felt like finally learning the language and then spending the next year doing whatever grunt work is asked of you to build relationships with the national church.

So why does God get us pumped up to do what He asks of us and then bid us to wait after we answer the call? Maybe it's because we need something more than passion. Maybe something happens in the time in between that doesn't happen at any other time.

His brow crumpled in disappointment as he approached me. He wanted the two-seat row to himself. I'm not going to lie. I was equally upset. As he put his carry-on in the overhead bin, I turned to the window. If I pretended he wasn't there, we'd both almost get our wish of being alone.

Talk to him.

No way, God. Not this time. I'm tired. I've had an emotional trip. I miss my family.

Talk to him.

I turned to my neighbor with a sigh. "So where are you headed?"

"Home to Atlanta," he answered disinterestedly. "You?"

"Home to Hanoi." Suddenly he seemed a little more interested. He'd traveled to Thailand for a "wild bachelor party," and he'd always wanted to visit Vietnam.

The plane began to take off, and my new acquaintance grabbed his head. In a pained voice, he explained to me that he'd been having problems with his ears and that he'd passed out on his last flight. A moan of pain interrupted our conversation and blood dripped from his ear.

Surely the Holy Ghost could have come immediately. Surely Pentecost could have happened the moment the apostles gathered in the Upper Room. And yet something happened in the waiting. No, not with God. He isn't slow. He doesn't need convincing. He surely can't be rushed. No, we see it throughout the Bible. David was anointed long before he took the throne. The Children of Israel wandered the desert well after the land had been promised to them. Joseph went from favored son to slave to prisoner before the prophetic dream God had given him was realized. Something seems to happen within those who wait.

We're just waiting, but God—who sees everything, loves everyone, and wants all people to know Him, who is always moving—is doing something. Why? Maybe because in the times we are forced to separate ourselves, we are forced to focus on God, and something happens. We hear Him more clearly in the calm. We seek Him more fervently in the waiting. We respond more readily in the time in between.

I turned back to the window and whispered, "God please touch this man's ear." The words were sincere and simple. I didn't want to cause a stir, so I made my plea to God while facing the small airplane window, then turned to see if the prayer was answered.

My neighbor's head jerked toward mine at the same time, and, in his eyes, I saw something like shock. "Were you praying for me?" I nodded, trying to discern whether he was angry or surprised. "It worked!"

I believe the apostles wouldn't have experienced Pentecost had they not waited in the Upper Room, as my new friend wouldn't have been healed if not for my wait. Waiting is as much an act of obedience as anything else. If I would have been on my original plane to a different city, this man wouldn't have experienced the miraculous power of a God who cared enough to rearrange my day, reach into an airplane, and heal him. I would have chosen to sleep in my own row with a more convenient travel schedule, but God's way was better. It always is.

ANSWER THE CALL

- Occasionally, God allows us to see what He has been doing during our times of waiting. How do these occasions help us handle the times when we can't see?

  _____

  _____

  _____

  _____

  _____

- Are you willing to be inconvenienced and wait so that God might work through you?

  _____

  _____

  _____

  _____

  _____

GO WAIT!

Next time you are inconvenienced, have to wait, or your plans are upended, spend the time talking to God. Ask Him to give you patience and to use you. Then listen for His voice and follow His leading.

PRAY

Never Reached People Group: VANUATU'S NORTHERN SA

Ask God to raise up intercessors with a heart for the Northern Sa.

Seasons of Buildup

By Joel Hoobyar, Indonesia

Weeds and thorns grow quickly. The good stuff takes time.

Waiting is a season of going.

The president of a missions organization once told me, "It took my wife and me 32 years to produce four children. It took us another 20 for our kids to multiply into seven. Don't ever get discouraged about how long it takes for you to see fruit in your life."

For some divine reason, God has engineered seasons of buildup as a part of nature. We see this in the way that clouds take up water before they can pour down rain. We see this in the development of a small seed into a leafy tree. As a gardener living in the tropics, I've been able to observe that few desirable plants grow rapidly. Weeds and thorns grow quickly. The good stuff takes time.

Waiting goes against our nature. But it's part of God's plan. He told His disciples:

"Do not leave Jerusalem, but wait for the gift my Father promised" (Acts 1:4, NIV).

Sooner or later, we all must wait. Not only does this go against our preferences, it also seems to conflict with Jesus' command to "go into all the world and make disciples." Should we wait or should we go? We all come to such crossroads in our lives. Is God's plan for me now a season of productivity or a season of buildup? To know, we must be familiar with the Lord's voice.

The Lord will make our next steps clear when we spend time in His presence on a daily basis. In fact, in the incubator of constant prayer, disciples receive more than they're looking for. Three fruits result from seasons of buildup:

1. *Character.* Just as roots make a tree stable, so seasons of buildup produce men and women of God who are spiritually stable. In seasons of waiting, we can develop godly habits and consistency. Many people have no patience for developing such fruit. They want to see results immediately. Without spiritual stability, the next type of fruit is often misused.

2. *Power.* Because the disciples chose to wait, their focus sharpened. They'd spent 10 days looking upward, so when the power from on high came down, they were looking in the right direction. They were ready to use this power. In fact, Acts 2:11 says they were

"declaring the wonders of God." Immediately, without someone teaching them how, they used this power to exalt God. God was undeniably doing something powerful. This produced the third fruit of waiting:

3. *Open doors.* Not only had the disciples been seasoned and empowered, God opened a door for them to proclaim the good news. Peter boldly addressed the crowd. He clearly explained their need to repent and that the power of the Holy Spirit was available to all. That day, the church grew by 2,600 percent!

One of the hardest things to do as a Christian is to wait upon the Lord. As a fresh graduate of Bible school with a call to the mission field, I was ready to save the world. But God told me something similar to what Jesus spoke to His disciples: to remain in my city and put down roots in the local church. I obeyed and began serving faithfully. After a few years, I grew antsy and met with my pastor. I told him I'd been fasting, and it was clear to me that I was supposed to serve oversees with a friend in North Africa. It all made sense to me. But God was still developing character in me, and my pastor helped me see that. We put the brakes on what I'd determined was my time to go. I'm so thankful that I didn't push past his counsel. I spent another three years in that church. Not only did God develop character in me, but he also gave me a wife. Now that's power! God opened doors, and within nine months of starting to raise our budget, we were on the field. God's still opening doors.

One of the most remarkable things about the story of Pentecost was that the disciples obeyed. Although Jerusalem was the headquarters of the Jewish leaders who crucified Jesus, the disciples didn't skip the process and head back to their comfort zone at home in Galilee. They stayed put. God had ordained a specific season of buildup for them, and when that buildup was complete, power flowed freely to them.

Imagine being the guy who decided to head back to his hometown and missed that first Pentecost. God sometimes calls us to seasons of buildup. Yes, He propels us into seasons of intense activity and fruitfulness, but these are nearly always preceded by seasons of buildup. Just like a caterpillar must eat its fill and cocoon itself before taking wing as a butterfly, so we must never shun the process of taking in the power of God that allows us to burst into true fulfillment of God's call.

When was the last time you waited in obedience to God? God chooses to speak loudest in seasons of waiting. Quiet yourself and hear God speak. Allow Him to develop lasting character in you, character that will become fertile soil for power from on high. God will open wide the doors for you to carry that power into the next season of your life and beyond the borders of your imagination. Never miss the power of Pentecost because you were too busy to receive.

ANSWER THE CALL

- Are you in a season of buildup or fruit bearing?

_____

_____

_____

_____

_____

- What is God developing in you to use in going and telling others about Christ?

_____

_____

_____

_____

_____

GO WAIT!

Spiritual power proceeds from waiting in God's presence. Commit to spending time seeking the Lord for your own personal Pentecost and renewed power to witness in your home town, your nation, and to the ends of the earth. And in the waiting, never lose sight of the end goal—going to the ends of the earth as a witness for Christ.

PRAY

Never Reached People Group: THE MADURA OF INDONESIA

Pray that God will raise up and empower believers from Madura to build a strong church to reach their own people.

NOTES

NOTES

NOTES

NOTES

NOTES

NOTES

NOTES